Α.Γ. ΜΕΤΑΞΑΣ
ΑΡΧΙΤΕΚΤΩΝ ΤΩΝ ΑΘ

# PALACES
## IN GREECE

PUBLICATION CO-ORDINATION   Annie Ragia

TRANSLATION   David Hardy

TEXT EDITING   Michael Eleftheriou

FINAL EDITING   Dimitris Philippides

PAGINATION   Kelly Kalogirou, Theoni Soupiona

REPRODUCTION OF ILLUSTRATIONS   Kostas Adam

PRINTING   EPIKOINONIA

BINDING   Giorgos Iliopoulos


ISBN   978-960-204-2892


© copyright 2009, MELISSA Publishing House
58 Skoufa St., Athens 106 80, T. 210/3611692, F. 210/3600865
www.melissabooks.com

MARO KARDAMITSI-ADAMI

# PALACES IN GREECE

PHOTOGRAPHS
YIORGIS YEROLYMBOS

NATIONAL HISTORICAL MUSEUM
MELISSA PUBLISHING HOUSE

# CONTENTS

# A GREETING

It is with great pleasure that I greet the publication of this study by Professor Maro Kardamitsi-Adami, which was undertaken by Melissa Publications with the support and cooperation of the Historical and Ethnological Society of Greece.

A significant number of the drawings included in this study come from the old and varied collections that, together, formed King George I's personal archive and which were brought together to form a museum in their own right before World War Two. When this museum ceased to operate, the material was handed over in perpetuity to the National Historical Museum to be safeguarded, studied and displayed in conjunction with the Museum's wealth of other exhibits.

The drawings illustrating in this book from the Museum's collections concern the palaces, villas and ancillary structures that were actually built for the Greek royal family, including Tatoi and Mon Repos, but also those buildings and projects –such as the conversion of the Petalioi islands into a royal resort, and the little palace in Tripoli– that were designed but never implemented.

This volume is especially useful because it furnishes a picture of the plans and aspirations of the royal court and supplements our knowledge of the rationale underlying official architectural programmes in Greece, primarily during the 19th century.

We would like to extend our most heartfelt thanks to the book's author, Mrs M. Kardamitsi-Adami, who had the knowledge and experience required to undertake the presentation of the architectural drawings designs included herein. We would also like to thank Melissa Publications for, once again, providing the reading public with a work of academic value and aesthetic beauty. With their help, the Historical and Ethnological Society of Greece has now completed the study and publication of an important section of its collections and its presentation to a broader public for further study.

**Ioannis Mazarakis-Ainian**
General Secretary of the Historical
and Ethnological Society of Greece

*To the memory of my parents*
*Marios and Pitsa Kardamitsis*

# INTRODUCTORY NOTE

I embarked on this project several years ago, when I was asked by the Ethnological and Historical Museum to examine and identify a number of drawings, including the designs for the palace at Tripoli. Some time later, Aliki Solomou showed me the drawings that are now kept in the King George I Archive, again at the Ethnological and Historical Museum. According to Ioulia Karolou, a lady-in-waiting to Queen Olga, these were presented to the Historical and Ethnological Society of Greece to be exhibited in the King George I Museum, which was to be built in the National Gardens. The designs, which were never implemented, were for palaces on Petalioi, at Tatoi and in Piraeus and included a number of other drawings for smaller ancillary buildings which were ultimately built at Tatoi. All of them had been completely neglected for some seventy-five years; it was only much later, in 2004, that the drawings for Tatoi were published by Kostas Stamatopoulos.

In February 1999, as part of the advanced seminar in the History of Architecture given by Professor C. Bouras at the National Technical University of Athens, my colleague Natalia Boura and I published a preliminary presentation of the designs relating to the palaces built for the Glücksburgs (as opposed to older branches of the House of Schleswig-Holstein) in Greece. Since then, I have continued my research and extended it to cover other 19th-century designs for palaces in Greece some of which were built, others not.

Not all the information presented in this volume is new, of course. Extensive, well-documented monographs have been written on Gärtner's palaces in Athens, on Tatoi and on Mon Repos by Aikaterini Demenegi-Viriraki, Kostas Stamatopoulos and Sissy Kyriaki respectively. Much, too, has been written about Schinkel and Klenze's unimplemented designs for the Athens palace, the Queen's Tower in Chaidari (Liossia), Theophilus Hansen's unrealised proposal for the palace in Piraeus, and the palace of saints Michael and George and the Achilleion on Corfu. In all these cases, however, there is always something new to be added, something new to be said.

The present volume includes what I believe to be the first detailed accounts of L. Lange's unimplemented design for King Otto's palace, Christian Hansen's proposal for the country palace of George I, also unrealised, the designs for the palaces on Petalioi and at Tatoi by E. Ziller and E.H. Piat, another unidentified proposal for the palace in Piraeus, and Ziller's drawings for the Crown Prince's palace (now the Presidential Mansion).

I believe that this will represent the first comprehensive account of 19th-century palaces in Greece and pave the way for further monographs.

The architectural material presented is from: the George I Archive in the Historical and Ethnological Museum, the Ziller Archive in the Greek National Gallery, the Savvas Boukis Archive, the Benaki Museum Neohellenic Architecture Archive, the National (Royal) Theatre of Athens Archive, the National Vallianeios Library, the Athens General State Archives, the Theophilus Hansen Archive in the Vienna School of Fine Arts, the Karl Friedrich Schinkel Archive, the Leo von Klenze and Lange archives in the State Graphic Arts Collection in Munich, the Gärtner Archive at Munich Technical University, and private collections.

I should like to extend my thanks to Constantine, the former king of Greece; to Natalia Boura, Aliki Solomou, Marilena Kasimati, Aristea Papanikolaou-Christensen, Evridiki Ambatzi, Maria Gerokostopoulou, Vivi Vasilopoulou and Anna Kotsovili; to Ioannis and Philippos Mazarakis-Ainian, Kostas Stamatopoulos, Giorgos Panetsos, Vasilis Kaskouras and Takis Gavriil for the valuable help they have provided in one way or another. Thanks also to the colleagues and friends with whom I have from time to time discussed related matters, and who have helped me to clarify my thinking. There are many of them.

I am very grateful to my friend and colleague Yiorgis Yerolymbos, who has once again enhanced the text with his superb photographs. Finally, I would like once more to thank the Ragia family, and Annie Ragias in particular, for embracing my idea and giving me the opportunity to turn thoughts into actions.

Maro Kardamitsi-Adami

1. *Dionysios Tsokos,* The assassination of Ioannis Kapodistrias, *Communità Greco-Orientale, Trieste.*

# INTRODUCTION

There were palaces in Greece from prehistory. The first palaces were undoubtedly those inhabited by the twelve gods on Mount Olympos, but no trace of these would appear to have survived. Much more is known about the palaces at Knossos, Phaestos, Mycenae and Tiryns.

During the Byzantine period, the emperor dwelt in the sacred *palation* in Constantinople. The Greek *palation* is from the Latin *palatium*, which is in turn derived from the name of the Palatine Hill in Rome on which the emperor Augustus built his palace.

Very few palaces are mentioned in Greece during its time as a province (*or theme*) of the Byzantine empire. Byzantine architecture sought primarily to glorify the Church and demonstrate to the entire world how the teachings of Christ were now embodied in the omnipotent, hierarchic, sacred and divine institution of empire. Byzantine architecture is pre-eminently ecclesiastical, and has produced some of the finest religious structures ever constructed.

The Venetians, Franks, Catalans and the Ottoman Turks who ruled Greece after the fall of Constantinople focused their efforts on building impregnable fortresses to reinforce their dominion over their respective domains and paid less attention to the erection of palaces. There were, of course, large mansions and *serai*, but these were certainly no match in size or opulence for palaces in the Western world during the same period.

The history of the modern Greek state effectively begins on 6 July 1827 with the signing of the Treaty of London. Although it remained doubtful whether the treaty would actually be implemented throughout the autumn and winter of that year, the map of Europe had now changed: Greece had at last taken its place among the other states of Europe. However, it would be a long time before the rights and borders of the new state were firmly established.

One thing, however, was clear: Greece had no suitably palatial residence to offer its new governor. Everything had to be built from scratch. When the British frigate *Warspit* set sail from Malta for Greece on 2 January 1828, it had the first governor of Greece aboard, Count Ioannis Kapodistrias of Corfu, who was already in the fifty-second year of his life. The governor landed at Nafplion before continuing to Aegina, where he took up residence.

Born on Corfu to a family listed in the island's Libro d'Oro, Kapodistrias had grown up in aristocratic circles. In both his native land and in Russia, where he served in the tsar's court, initially as a member of the diplomatic corps and later as foreign minister, he lived and was entertained as a guest in notable mansions and palaces. When he accepted the post of governor of Greece, he entertained no illusions about the condition of the country. Having resigned his position as foreign minister to the tsar, a resignation that was duly accepted in the summer of 1822, he knew what was ahead of him. Still, the reality may well have been even worse than he had imagined, though, as he noted shortly after his appointment: "the road of our life is preordained; we have no choice"; it was clear the road was neither strewn with roses nor ran alongside palaces.

Kapodistrias' strict political line, which sought to create as independent a state as possible, was not to the liking of the Great Powers. The events that followed are known to all: Kapodistrias was assassinated in September 1831. Then, after a year of intense round-table and back-room negotiations, twelve representatives from Greece –including three heroes of the Greek War of Independence: Plapoutas, Botsaris and Miaoulis– travelled to Munich where, speaking in the name of the Greek people, they expressed their confidence in the new king chosen by the plenipotentiaries of the three Great Powers. The document was signed by the Elector of Bavaria, amongst others, on 29 April 1832, and ratified on 27 July of the same year by the Greek National Assembly at Pronoia. Greece now had a king, and the king would be needing a palace in which to live.

# AEGINA

## GOVERNMENT HOUSE (UNCLE JOHN'S LITTLE)

**2.** Ioannis Kapodistrias:
detail from a ceiling painting.

**3.** Aegina: Government House.
Early 20th century. Postcard.

**A**egina's capital was a small town that had only come into being in the late 18th century; naturally, it lacked a suitable mansion. Generally speaking, Aegina town was shoddily-built with narrow alleyways and a paucity of large houses. The government committee decided to repair one of them –the mansion built by Archimandrite Grigorios Maras, in which Petrobey Mavromichalis had taken up temporary residence– and make it available to the governor.

The L-shaped house was large by the standards of the island, with two storeys and a tiled roof. Today, the ground floor consists of nine small interconnecting rooms; the upper storey of an entrance hall and four large rooms. There were four entrances and an external marble staircase leading up to the first floor where Kapodistrias' living quarters are believed to have been located. The refurbishment was undertaken by Theodoros Vallianos of Cephalonia, an officer in Tsar Alexander's Engineering Corps who had sailed to Greece immediately after the proclamation of the War of Independence to offer his services.

The precise modifications made by Vallianos to the original building are not known. A study of the present structure has revealed several building phases that are difficult to date with accuracy, primarily because the building has undergone numerous subsequent conversions and changes of use ever since. All we know is that the Governor's instructions, as conveyed to Aegina by his servant Nikoletos, who supervised the refurbishment and "determined the necessary subdivisions of the rooms", were that they should be confined to the essential.

"One day", the freedom fighter Kasomoulis writes in his memoirs, "I toured the rooms with General Petros Mavromichalis out of curiosity, and so very small did they seem that I did not consider them in keeping with his dignity. Indeed, imagining that he would be receiving large number of visitors, as is the custom among us, I remarked on their confinedness to his servant. He replied to me that they were spacious enough". Mavromichalis adds: "They did not leave him as much as a cupboard. Where would he keep his sweets, or the rum he would be offering his guests? Where was the table around which we would dine together?". According to contemporary accounts, the Governor's only table was the desk at which he wrote or dictated to his secretaries on administrative matters from morning until late at night. No balls or dinners were held in "Uncle John's little palace", as the Governor's residence was known locally. The sixteen chests containing Kapodistrias' luxurious household effects –porcelain crockery, glassware, silver, lace, velvet and precious carpets– were left unopened, both on Aegina and in Nafplion when he moved to the mainland. Indeed, they remained closed until the day of his assassination, after which they were taken to Corfu by his brothers. A detailed inventory of their contents reveals extravagant items befitting the tsar's foreign minister, including crystal port and champagne glasses. The only chests opened were those containing his library – some 2,000 volumes in French, Italian, German, Russian, English and, of course, Greek. Frugal and austere, Kapodistrias did not wish to affront the Greek people, who had still to recover from their ongoing struggle for independence.

A few months later, the Governor took up residence in Nafplion. The building on Aegina remained empty, but was used by Kapodistrias on his brief visits to the island. However, following his assassination in September 1831, the building was abandoned and ceded to the diocese of Aegina in 1839 or 1846 to serve as the bishop's residence. Having undergone a number of changes of use, "Uncle John's little palace" now houses the Aegina Historical Archives.

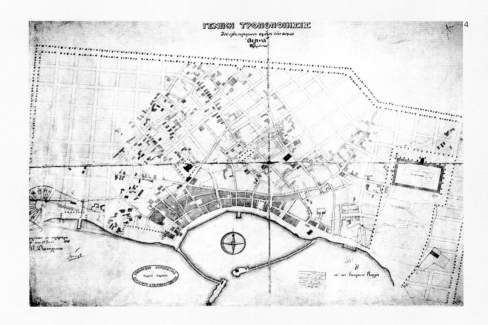

**4**. *Aegina: map of Aegina town. 1898. Hellenic Ministry for Urban Planning and the Environment archive.*

# NAFPLION

## THE LITTLE PALACE

5. *J. Stieler,* King Otto of Greece. *1832.*

6. *Peter von Hess,* King Otto arriving in Nafplio. *1835.*

**T**he Governor's second residence, in Nafplion, is referred to variously as the 'Palace', 'Government House' and the 'Little Palace'. Like "Uncle John's Little Palace" on Aegina, it (or part of it, at least) was an existing building – in this case, a three-storey house owned by a Turkish agha, Isis Moskov Huseyinoglu, a 'born and bred' Nafpliot who fled the town after its capture by the Greeks and settled in Smyrna. The house was bought by the government to serve as the governor's residence.

The alterations and refurbishment were undertaken by Pasquale Hippolyte, an architect serving as a non-commissioned officer in the Engineering Corp, under the supervision of generals Piza and Vallianos. It would appear from the surviving documentation that repair work began in March 1829 and was completed late in the same year or early in the following.

According to the plans of Nafplion drawn up by Stamatis Voulgaris and Stade-mann in 1828 and 1834 respectively, the building had a trapezoid ground plan (approximately 9 by 30 metres) whose longer side gave onto Trion Navarchon Square, the square in the new neoclassical town designed by Voulgaris.

Nafplion's Little Palace was an early example of the neoclassical style. Its main three-storey façade was divided into three vertical sections. The central section, which protruded slightly from the rest of the building, was emphasised by a balcony on the second floor and a central gateway on the ground floor with an alley through it. The building was also divided horizontally into a clearly-delineated base, main section and crown.

A watercolour from 1834 by Adalbert Marc, and the famous painting by Peter von Hess, who sailed to Greece with the Bavarian forces and immortalised King Otto's arrival in the country, both indicate that the palace was light blue in colour, with vertical bands and horizontal string courses in white.

The form of the building, divided into two by the main gate on the ground floor, recalls corresponding examples of Venetian –and, in general, Italian– architecture. Like the buildings on the long side of Trion Navarchon Square on Vasileos Konstantinou Street, it probably dates from Nafplion's second Venetian period. It is not impossible, however, that Hippolyte linked two originally separate buildings to the right and left of the alley passing beneath the main gate. The entrance to the palace was by way of this small portico. The building was burned to the ground in 1929, exactly 100 years after it was converted into a palace. Contemporary descriptions of its interior reveal a frugal, austere building. "We crossed a deserted street and entered a house whose exterior had nothing special about it. I don't recall even seeing a guard at the entrance", writes Joseph Michaud, a French traveller who accompanied Rouan, the French ambassador, on a visit to Kapodistrias in 1830. He goes on: "We passed along a narrow, gloomy corridor (he presumably means the entrance portico), and ascended a wooden staircase, bringing us into an antechamber, where no one was to be found. Plainness on this scale reminded me to some extent of the ancient virtues of Greece, and, if you had been there, you would have thought that I was going to visit Phokion or a Stoic philosopher.

The Governor received us in a fairly large room, where the light entered on all sides, and in which the sun, so to speak, was the only adornment. The only furniture was a circular divan and a kind of desk at which the Governor worked".

The governor, "unmarried, with frugal habits, entirely devoted to the execution of his great duties, dwelt without ostentation and luxury, like the simplest of individuals, in his austere house", wrote Alexandros Rangavis in his memoirs. Apart from a large reception which he held in honour of the representatives of the three Great Powers soon after his arrival at Nafplion, Kapodistrias lived very modestly. As he himself writes in a letter to Count Lomverdos in Paris: "It is not true that I am inaccessible to the inhabitants even with regard to the official matters of which you speak. My room is open to all from morning until evening. But I do not show excessive favour to anyone, nor do I hold dinners, but nor do

7. Nafplio, Constitution Square. Painted by Grafner Ottobrunn, a Bavarian soldier. King Otto Museum.

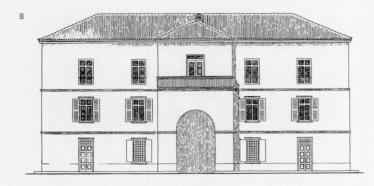

ΜΕΓΑΡΟΝ ΚΑΠΟΔΙΣΤΡΙΟΥ.     ΝΑΥΠΛΙΟΝ. 863.

I do any of those things which, pandering to expressions of vanity and whims, are completely alien to my moral code".

Despite the frugality of the governor and of the 'palace' itself, its location on the main axis of Trion Navarchon Square gave it the requisite prestige and gravity. Despite its dimensions and imposing, majestic style, Nafplion's other large public building, in the Venetian arsenal in Platanou (now Syntagma) Square, served as a barracks in the early years of the Greek state, and the garrison used the square in front of it for drilling.

The Greek town-planner Stamatis Voulgaris, an officer in the French Army and a personal friend of Kapodistrias, accompanied him on his journey from Malta to Greece and was commissioned to draw a town plan for Nafplion. Voulgaris may well have deliberately avoided using the large Venetian building: when designing the town of Nafplion and dividing the city into neighbourhoods, he decided where new public institutions should be built. The town was badly built, in his view, and partly ruined, so he took the opportunity to trace a new street plan and to create larger and more regular squares and streets on sites provided by ruined houses. Next to the moat that divided the peninsula of Nafplion from the rest of the Argolid, he planned a tree-lined avenue running parallel with the town walls from the Land Gate to the town's central square, which he named Trion Navarchon Square and where he sited the new palace. The Venetian arsenal, according to S. Voulgaris, with the "Bucentaur, so artfully engraved and richly gilded, which the Venetians still show with pride in their great shipyard, and which recalls the pomp and majesty of their festivals, their luxurious way of life, and the cause of their decline", was certainly not the most appropriate structure for the new leadership to associate itself with.

This building, in which the young king Otto lived when he first moved to Greece, became known as the 'Royal Palace', and the street on which it stood was called Odos Palatiou [Palace Street]. According to L. Ross, Otto later wrote about this "cosy, humble little house" to his father, King Ludwig of Bavaria, saying that "although the rooms are not very large, they are comfortable and spacious and

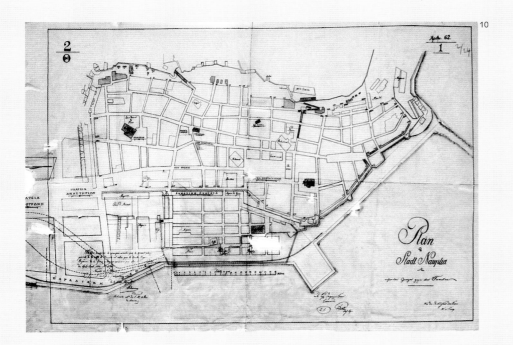

8. *Nafplio, the Little Palace. Drawn by W. Schaefer. 1935. German Archaeological Institute.*

9. *Nafplio, the Little Palace: the narrow road leading to the rear of the building. Postcard.*

10. *F. Stademann's city plan for Nafplio. 1834. Hellenic Ministry for Urban Planning and the Environment archive.*

11. *Trion Navarchon square with the Little Palace in the background. Painted by Marc Adalbert, 1834.*

made a pleasant impression on me. In my opinion, the best living conditions involve comfortable rooms with the walls agreeably covered, a good view, and a clear sky". Young Greece may not have been able to offer the 17-year-old king a sumptuous, majestic palace, but it certainly had a clear blue sky. However, while the experienced politician Ioannis Kapodistrias worked from morning till night in his study as he struggled to create a soundly-organised Greek state out of chaos, the young Otto left the complexities of state affairs to his regents– to Count Armansberg, in particular– as he strove to prepare himself at Maurer's side for the difficult role awaiting him. While Count Armansberg governed, Otto took Maurer's daughters riding or played blind man's buff with them, and danced away his Saturday evenings at balls which the regent held in his 'salon'. At the same time, he was learning Greek and trying to familiarize himself with the people he was to govern: the Greeks.

A few years later, when the royal seat was transferred to Athens, which had been declared the nation's capital in 1834, Otto left Nafplion for Athens.

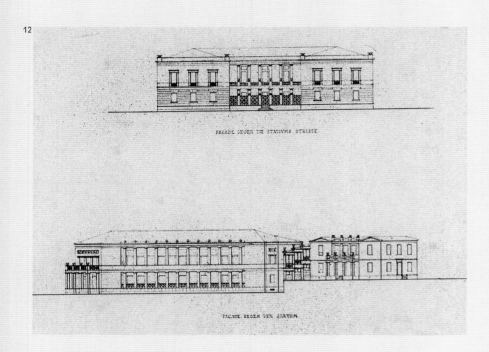

FACADE GEGEN DIE STADIUMS STRASSE.

FACADE GEGEN DEN GARTEN.

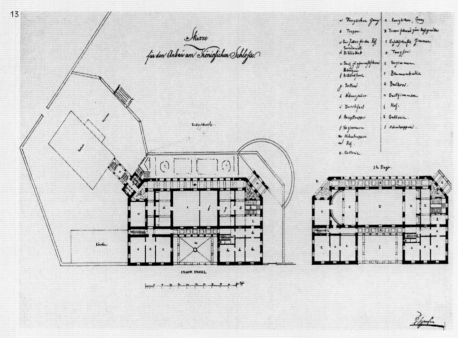

## OTTO'S FIRST ATHENIAN RESIDENCES

### THE MEGARON OF KONTOSTAVLOS

lthough Nafplion had a palace, albeit small and humble, to accommodate the king, there was no equivalent found in the new capital, which had only recently (1831) shaken off the Ottoman yoke. A certain "catalogue of houses in Athens which may be made available to the government and its servants" contains only seventy-three buildings, most of them with two or three rooms at most. Typical Athenian homes of the Ottoman period, they were small and simple single- or two-storey buildings with a garden, a courtyard and an L- or U-shaped *hagiati* [covered veranda]. The few large buildings were all recently erected: the house of the British historian George Finlay at the intersection of Adrianou and Hill Streets, a two-storey structure

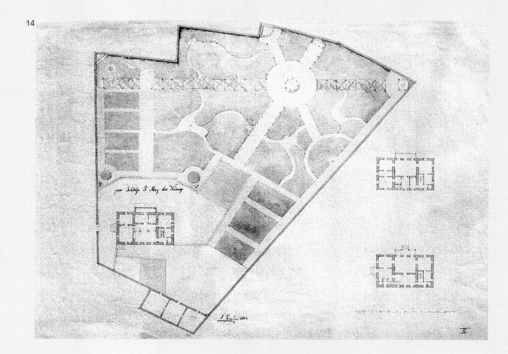

**12, 13.** *C. Hansen. The Kontostavlos Mansion: proposed enlargement. Elevations and floor plans for the ground and upper storeys. 1834. Munich. State Drawing and Print Collection.*

**14.** *C. Hansen. The Kontostavlos Mansion. Site plan. 1834. Munich. State Drawing and Print Collection.*

surrounded by a large garden; the Vlachoutsis residence on Peiraios Street, another two-storey structure in which the regent, Count Armansberg, took up residence; the house of Count Botsaris in Kapnikareas Square; and the Megaron of Kontostavlos which would later become Greece's first Parliament and now houses the Historical and Ethnological Museum.

Almost immediately after the liberation of Athens, Alexandros Kontostavlos, a Chiot, who collaborated with Kapodistrias in the economic sphere and was one of the first to settle in the new capital, assigned the task of building his residence to Stamatis Kleanthis and Eduard Schaubert, architects he had met on Aegina. The Megaron of Kontostavlos was possibly the first neoclassical building to be erected in Athens. An architectural drawing which Christian Hansen made in 1834 gives us a precise idea of its form: a two-storey neoclassical mansion. It recalls similar villas by the German architect Karl Friedrich Schinkel tutor of both Kleanthis and Schaubert.

Although relatively small and simple in form, the building was not lacking in monumentality and did not fail to make an impression on the Athenians, who greeted the new building with the satirical couplet:

*From afar, Kontostavlos, your house*

*looks like an American frigate,*

*which, after all, is what paid for it.*

This was a pointed illusion to the fact that throughout the Greek War of Independence Kontostavlos had been seconded to Admiral Cochrane, who had just returned from America to negotiate the possible purchase of military frigates. These satirical verses did not influence the government, of course, which bought the building in 1834 from the Chiot, who was generally known to be an honourable man, to serve as Otto's palace.

The Megaron of Kontostavlos was just outside the old town, Plaka, without being too far away from it. Standing on Stadiou Street, the large boulevard which connected two of the apexes –modern Omonoia and Syntagma Squares– of the basic triangle of the town plan drawn up for Athens by Kleanthis and Schaubert, it stood between the Palace and the Bishop's Residence.

15. *F. Stademann. The octagonal ballroom and the Kontostavlos Mansion. Detail of Panel no. 10 from the "Panorama". 1841. Munich.*

16. *The octagonal ballroom and the Kontostavlos Mansion. Lithograph from the Royal Printing Press. 1838. Private collection.*

17. *Letter relating to the purchase of carriages for King Otto.*
*General State Archives, Royal Palace Archive.*

Set in a large garden, the neoclassical mansion stood at an oblique angle to Stadiou Street and at right angles to Voulis Street. Its main façade looked onto the garden which extended as far as what is now Anthimou Gazi Street. This meant that it had its back to Stadiou Street and overlooked the square with the Bishop's Residence. It also and enjoyed an uninterrupted view of the Acropolis.

The façade of the building was divided into three parts. Its central section protrubed slightly from the rest and was emphasised by a balcony on the first floor. The horizontal articulation of the composition served to draw attention to its division into base, main body and crown. A horizontal decorative band encircled the building between the two storeys. The modifications required to make it suitable for a royal residence were carried out between October 1834, when the building was purchased, and 1 December, when Otto took up residence.

According to a memorandum now kept in the General State Archives, the building to be chosen as a residence for the king had to offer the following rooms:

A. The living quarters of H.M. the king:

1) bedroom, 2) study, 3) reception room, 4) service room for the adjutants, 5) dining room, 6) coffee room which will also be used as a music room, a chapel and an audience room; 7) valet's room, 8) service room for the domestic staff 9) wardrobe.

B. Ancillary rooms:

1) room in which to keep the silver, crystal and porcelain (this had to be in the building in which the king resided), 2) pastry kitchen, 3) kitchen with rooms for the cooks and a room for washing and storing vessels, 4) store room, 5) linen store with a room for sewing, ironing etc., 6) wine cellar, 7) cellar for the storage of items entrusted to the wine butler, 8) large storeroom for furniture, 9) wood and charcoal cellar.

This was followed by a list of staff quarters required (for the officials, secretaries, court musicians, pianist, doctor, pharmacists, priest, cooks, wine butler; doorman, servants etc.), as well as stables for thirty-six horses and six carriages with the appropriate staff. With regard to the carriages, it was recommended that

*Universal Wagen* be purchased, which had "the outstanding advantage of being convertible from closed to open vehicles and back again within two minutes and without incommoding the people within them in the slightest. These vehicles can be used for short trips, and also for travelling within and around a city". It was emphasised that similar vehicles were used by Grand Duchess Sophia and the Archduke of Austria, the emperor of Austria and Archduke Maximilian. "The cost of such a carriage is somewhere in the region of 1,400 florins".

The memorandum also specifies *inter alia* that the walls of the rooms were to be covered in light-blue silk (the national colour of both Greece and Bavaria) and that the rooms were to be suitably furnished.

When it was decided that Otto should reside in the mansion, the Danish Architect Christian Hansen, then serving in the Hellenic Foreign Ministry with the rank of Secretary Grade Two, carried out the study for the extension of the Kontostavlos residence.

The new building, which was about three times the size of the Megaron of Kontostavlos, was sited parallel to Stadiou Street and was intended to house Otto's secretarial staff as well as his retinue. Like the Megaron of Kontostavlos, which is named a palace on the architectural plan, it was oriented towards the garden and was directly linked with the palace by a portico. Its U-shaped plan created a small rectangular courtyard on the side facing Stadiou street –a kind of atrium enclosed on three sides– which afforded entrance to the public. The rear corners of the building were chamfered, making it possible to link it more closely to the palace. On the first floor of the building, a large rectangular hall opening onto a covered, arcaded veranda at the back of the building was to be used as a throne and reception room.

Generally speaking, the building retained the morphology of the Megaron of Kontostavlos, with which it formed a harmonious whole. It was suggested that a small church be built on the Stadiou Street side of the palace.

Hansen's design was never implemented.

In a letter written to his mother in May 1834, Hansen notes: "Since the decision was taken to make Athens the capital, among the other interesting events that

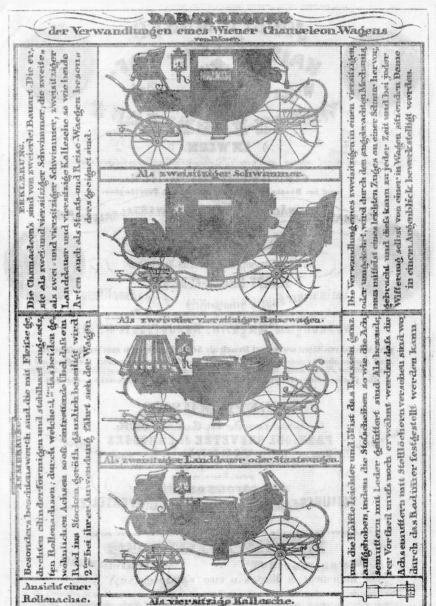

18. Universal Wagen *advertisement brochure. General State Archives, Royal Palace Archive.*

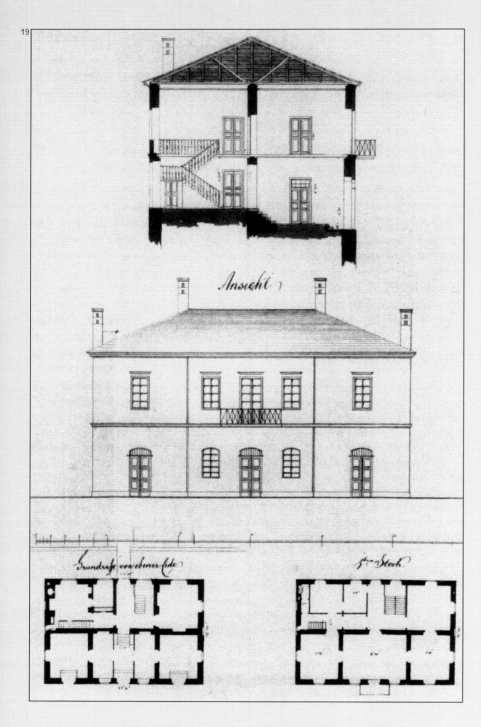

19

*Ansicht*

*Grundriss von ebener Erde*      *5ter Stock*

**19.** *G. Lüders and J. Hoffer. Plan of the Vouros Mansion. section, front elevation and plans. Museum of the City of Athens.*

**20.** *Leo von Klenze. Part of the Athens City Plan as it was officially approved in September 1834. Top left: the palace complex on Agios Athanasios Hill; Bottom centre: the Church of the Saviour (Omonoia Square). The Kontostavlos Mansion can also be made out. Benaki Museum, Neohellenic Architecture Archive.*

have taken place was the King ceremonially laying the corner stone of his palace; however, God alone knows when the other stones will be put in place. Meanwhile, one of Athens' mansions has been chosen as his temporary residence, with the further prospect of it becoming the home of the Hellenic Parliament when it is completed". The palace Hansen is referring to was the one that was to be built according to Kleanthis and Schaubert's original plans.

As early as 1833, however, Otto's brother Maximilian, heir to the throne of Bavaria, and Frederick Wilhelm, heir to the throne of Prussia, had commissioned Schinkel to design a palace on the Acropolis, while shortly afterwards, Leo von Klenze proposed transferring the royal palace from Omonoia Square to the site of the ancient cemetery of Kerameikos.

We shall return to Schinkel and Klenze's proposals below. Hansen's proposal was purely a makeshift solution, and was never intended as another alternative to the royal palace.

In place of the building designed by Hansen, a large octagonal ballroom was built in 1834 on the north side of the Megaron of Kontostavlos, to which it was linked "by three fine reception rooms", the work of the architect Röser. The octagonal hall was used as a throne room cum reception room, which replaced the first-floor room in Hansen's design. When the building was later converted to house the Hellenic Parliament, the octagonal room became an assembly room. Queen Amalia's maid of honour, Julie von Nordenflucht describes it thus: "As you know, the large banquet room in the other house consists of two separate structures, and is made with great refinement. The room is completely circular [she means internally], and is decorated with red silk hung between half-columns. The white ceiling is also covered with red cloth in places, and the two colours form a regular star in the centre. Five splendid chandeliers hang from the ceiling, and the one in the middle is to be replaced by a larger one with seventy candles. The windows have red curtains with fringes and tassels in white and red. The overall effect is most elegant and luxurious".

This view was not shared by the Danish author Hans Christian Andersen, who also described the room on his visit to Greece in 1841: "it is a room used for balls, and is in the shape of an octagonal rotunda with red wall-hangings and white curtains gathered together on the ceiling in a frightful rosette. There is also a monstrous chandelier, four smaller light fittings and six mirrors […] and a kind of altar which has been erected there. On the upper storey, the study of the heir to the throne, the prince of Bavaria, contains a large painting by Hess depicting the king's arrival in Nafplion […]". All in all, the temporary palace reminded Andersen of a "private country villa".

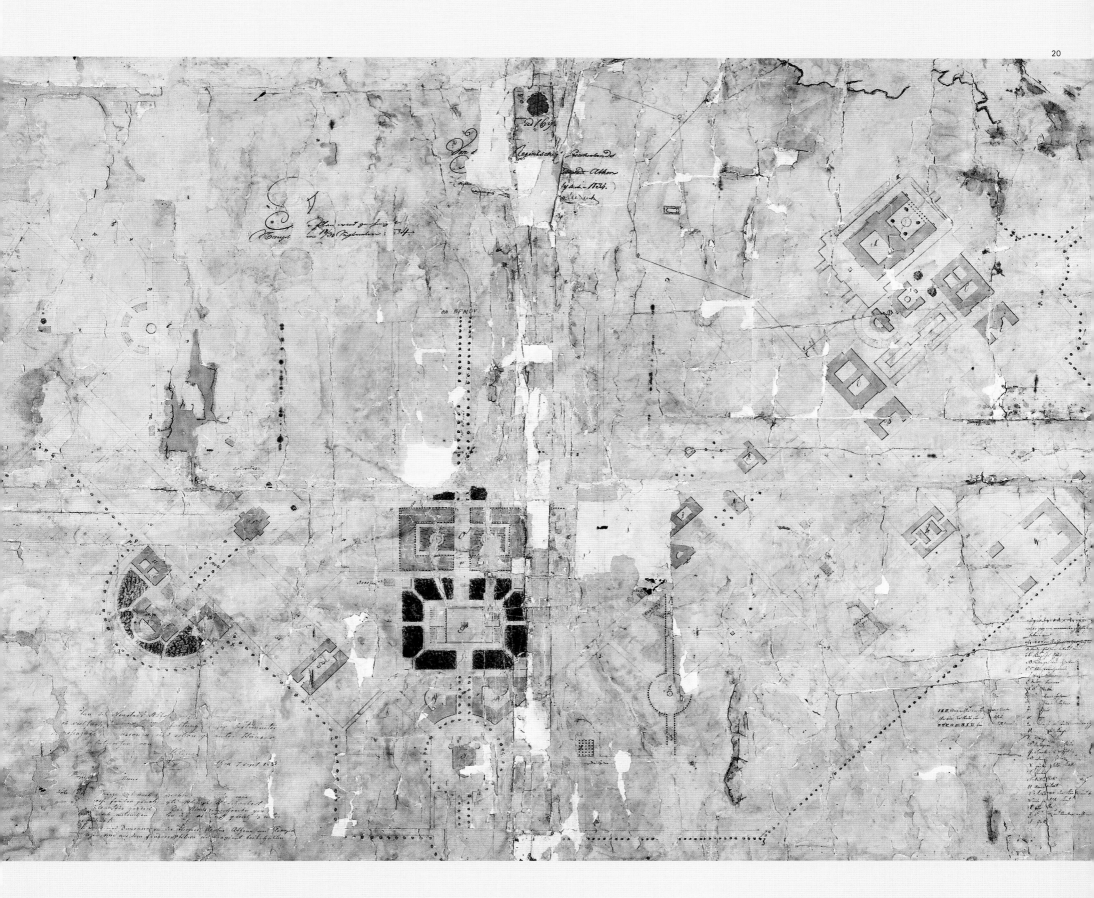

Hansen's proposal may not ultimately have been implemented, but a building had to be found near the palace to house his staff. To this end, the residence of the banker Stamatios Dekozis Vouros in Theatrou (now Klafthmonos) square was leased in 1834. Built in 1833 to designs by the architects G. Lüders and J. Hoffer, it was a typical example of a simple neoclassical building and very close to the Megaron of Kontostavlos.

After Otto took up residence in the temporary palace, the first Lord Chamberlain, Count Saportas, took strict charge of the royal court and laid down the rules of palace etiquette. Henceforth, the young prince would spend his mornings striving to familiarize himself with his duties and to get to know his people and their language, while his evenings would be dedicated to entertainment and participating in the social rituals of the capital. Receptions and balls were held both in the palace and in the regent's residence, which quickly became the epicentre of Athenian society and was, according to contemporary accounts, furnished and decorated in a luxurious fashion dictated by an interior decorator brought especially from Munich. At this stage, Athens 'society' consisted of Bavarian officials, the freedom fighters who had settled in the capital after the end of the Greek War of Independence, Phanariot families who had moved to Athens from Constantinople and a handful of aristocratic Athenian families. It took a long time for this very disparate group to knit together and form a homogeneous whole.

On 20 May 1835, Athens celebrated King Otto's coming of age with great solemnity. The ceremony, which was held in the Agia Eirini Cathedral and marked the end of the regency, was simple and austere. Ludwig had wanted an official coronation –for which a costly crown, sceptre and sword had been ordered from Paris– but his plans were scuppered by the Holy Synod's refusal to sanction the coronation of a non-Orthodox ruler with a religious service. The ceremony was followed by a reception at the palace.

A few months later, in the summer of the same year, Leo von Klenze arrived in Athens. Klenze, a distinguished architect and confidant of Ludwig of Bavaria, had come to Athens to amend the town plan drawn up by Kleanthis and

Schaubert and to rule on the site of the royal palace-to-be. On returning to Munich in the autumn, he drew up the final design for the palace, which, as we have seen, was to be sited in the Kerameikos area. In the meantime, however, von Klenze had fallen into disfavour with Ludwig. Although he retained his high office, his recommendations were not acted on.

A few months later, in December of the same year, King Ludwig of Bavaria came to Athens in person in the company of another architect, Friedrich von Gärtner, who had gained the king's favour as early as 1827 with designs he had drawn up for Ludwigstrasse. Ludwig's new favourite proposed yet another site for the erection of the palace: the third apex of the triangle in the Kleanthis-Schaubert plan, Mouson (now Syntagma) square, where the palace was ultimately built.

The foundation stone was laid on 6 February 1836, the third anniversary of Otto's arrival in Greece. Following a doxology in Athens' Agia Eirini Cathedral, kings Ludwig and Otto proceeded in procession to the site on which the palace was to be built. There, watched by 2,000 people from a small temporary amphitheatre erected especially for the event, Ludwig and Otto laid the corner stone of the future residence of the kings of Greece; the stone bore the inscription: "Mother earth, favourably receive me, the foundation stone of King Otto's home, 1834". Why 1834 and not 1836? Could this be the same stone that had been laid in Omonoia Square in March 1834: the corner stone of a palace that had never been built? This seems highly probable, particularly in view of the evidence suggesting that the stone came from the Acropolis. In keeping with the customary practice, the two kings also placed a few coins of Otto's realm in the foundations.

That same evening, this important event was marked by a ball in the palace to which Athens' dignitaries and notables were invited along with the diplomatic corps and a number of freedom fighters and their families. It was at this reception that Otto appeared in Greek dress ('fustanella') for the first time; Otto would wear a fustanella ever after, even in exile in Bavaria.

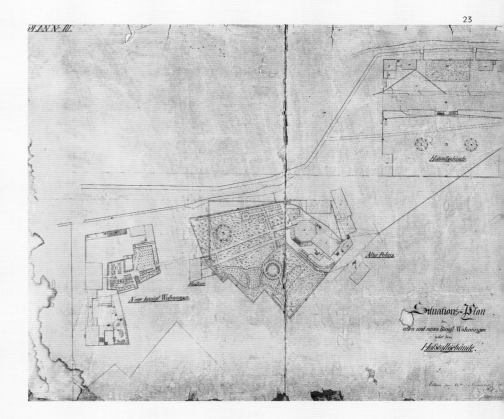

21. *G. Bodmer. Otto in Greek dress. 1835. Tinted lithograph.*

22. *Temporary palace. 1838. Royal Printing Press. Private collection.*

23. *Hoch. Plan of the old and new royal residences. 1837. Benaki Museum, Neohellenic Architecture Archive.*

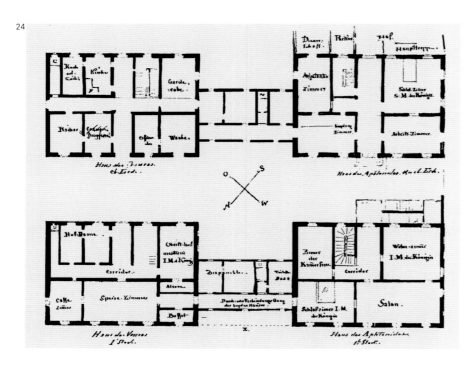

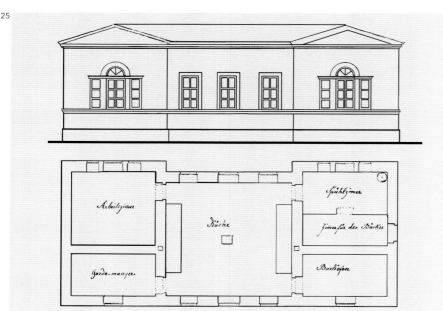

# THE VOUROS AND APHTHONIDIS
# RESIDENCES

**L**udwig returned to Bavaria in April 1836, followed six weeks later by Otto. Although the stated purpose of Otto's trip was to return his father's visit, his real purpose was to find a suitable bride amongst the noblewomen of his native land. The marriage of a king is not a private matter even today, far less so in the first half of the nineteenth century.

While Otto was away in Germany, the Vouros residence and the Aphthonidis residence next to it, which had been built in 1834-1836 and also housed some of the court services, were refurbished with a view to being joined and converted into an interim royal residence until the palace was built. At that point the Megaron of Kontostavlos was to be given to the state to house the Parliament and the Senate. The octagonal room would continue to be used as a reception room for a while. A small rectangular building –Mastronikolas House– was built

**24.** *The Vouros and Aphthonidis residences. Plan for their interconnection. General State Archives (File 238).*

**25.** *The Aphthonidis and Vouros residences. The kitchen. General State Archives (File 238).*

**26.** *Otto and Amalia. Coloured print.*

allowing for communication between the Vouros and Aphthonidis residences at the first-floor level by way of a passageway. It was in this small complex, which a contemporary engraving describes as a "temporary palace", that Otto and Amalia would spend the first years of their marriage.

Of the three buildings, the Vouros residence, a two-storey structure, is the most studiously built. Divided into three parts vertically, the central section is flanked by two brick pilasters that add interest to the façade. The central axis is emphasised by the main entrance, with its arched lintel, and by a first-floor balcony with finely wrought corbels and plain railings. A string course between the ground and first floors divides the building in two. The façade of the Aphthonidis residence is similarly designed, though its smaller dimensions obliged the architect to place its openings closer together, which diminishes its aesthetic effect, rendering it inferior to that of the Megaron residence. The unified structure is a typical example of early neoclassicism and the small, spare buildings of the era. Neither the ground plans nor the morphology of the façades are in any way comparable with those of the Megaron of Kontostavlos.

The Aphthonidis and Vouros residences were clearly intended from the outset to serve as a temporary residence for the royal couple alone. This is made absolutely clear both by the engraving printed by the Royal Press in 1888 and by the designs drawn up by the Bavarian architect, Hoch, in 1837 which label the former a "temporary palace" and the latter a "Plan for an Old and New royal residence".

Hoch's design, which is now held in the Benaki Museum Neohellenic Architecture Archive, contains detailed architectural drawings of the Megaron of Kontostavlos (with the addition of the octagonal ballroom), still in use after the royal couple moved into the "new royal residence", of its annexes and of the Vouros-Aphthonidis complex and the royal stables. The most interesting part of the design, however, is the detailed drawing of the gardens surrounding the buildings and the structure linking them.

A contemporary plan for the royal kitchens found in the Greek State Archives is in the same spirit. We do not, however, know whether the kitchens were ever built and if so where.

27. *The Vouros Residence today. The gate for the royal carriage.*

28. *The Vouros Residence today.*

**29.** *A. Haubenschid. King Otto's study in Athens. Hellenic Parliament Art Collection.*

**30.** *L. Lange. Ludwig I's room in Athens' temporary palace. 1836. Munich. State Drawing and Print Collection.*

**31.** *Vouros Residence. The throne room.*

**32.** *Vouros Residence. The staircase and the doorway leading into the courtyard.*

**33.** *Vouros Residence. Amalia's study.*

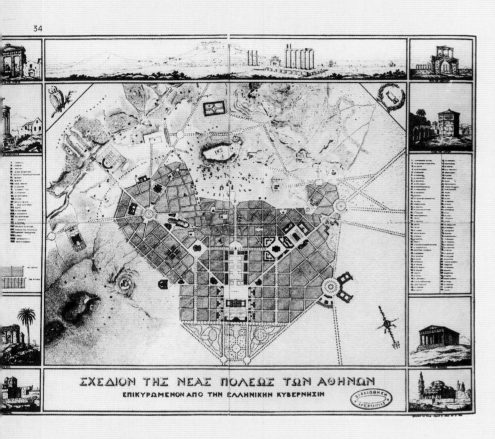

34

**34.** *S. Kleanthis and E. Schaubert. Athens City Plan in the form approved by the Greek government.*

## ATHEN'S ROYAL PALACES
## DESIGNS THAT WERE NEVER BUILT

The town plan of Athens and the location of the palace were, naturally enough, issues of concern to the architectural world and the Athenian society of the day as well as to latter-day scholars. Ultimately, it was Otto's father, King Ludwig of Bavaria, who played the key role in deciding where the royal palace was ultimately to be built.

## KLEANTHIS AND SCHAUBERT'S
## TOWN PLAN

In the Plan for Athens, drawn up by Kleanthis and Schaubert, the palace was located in Othonos (now Omonoia) square. Although no detailed drawings seem to have been drawn up for this palace, the town plan shows its outline. This consisted of a large rectangular enclosure to house the ancillary services and three solid blocks parallel to the short side of the rectangle, one being in the centre of the composition flanked by the other two; the structures are separated by two small and two large courtyards.

The models for these drawings are to be sought in similar palaces built in the same period or a few decades earlier in Europe, or in architectural handbooks such as the *Précis des leçons d'architecture* (1802-1805) by Jean-Nicolas-Louis Durand, a professor at the School of Architecture in Paris.

Professor Alexandros Papageorgiou-Venetas has provided a fairly free rendering of the palace in three-dimensional perspective in *Athens, a Vision of Classicism* in which he offers detailed comments of both the Plan of Athens and of the palace.

It is not clear whether Kleanthis or Schaubert ever proceeded with a more detailed plan. While Gottfried Böhm states in his *Aus der Zeit König Ludwigs* that the two architects had prepared a plan for the new king's palace, this has never been confirmed.

Ludwig of Bavaria assigned the project to experienced architects. The palace was important: the construction of a royal residence would give his son the prestige he required to establish himself firmly on the throne of Greece.

Despite the indubitable love and admiration for ancient Greece which had led Ludwig to assist the Greeks in their struggle to establish a modern Greek state, and despite his acception of the crown of the new kingdom as the guardian of his son Otto, who was still a minor, it should not be forgotten that this entire enterprise on the part of the Wittelsbach dynasty bore all the hallmarks of a utopian vision. Indeed, Ludwig himself had ascended to the throne of Bavaria –a kingdom founded after the dissolution of the Holy Roman German Empire in 1806 "by the grace of Napoleon", whose first king was his own father, Ludwig Maximilian I– only a few years earlier, in 1825. For the philhellene, art-loving Ludwig, who dreamed of creating a new classical city in his own capital, Munich, Athens was more than an aesthetic and artistic experience: it was an extension of his own kingdom.

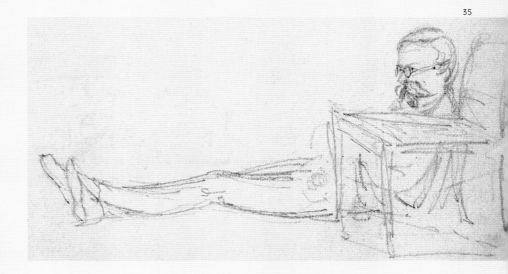

35

**35**. *C. Hansen. Sketch of S. Kleanthis (1802-1862). Copenhagen Academy of the Fine Arts.*

## A PALACE
## ON THE ACROPOLIS

It was evident to all obvious that the palace of the new king of Greece had to symbolize a vision. And there is no better proof of this than the superb designs for a palace on the Acropolis by Karl Friedrich Schinkel, the great German architect who taught both Kleanthis and Schaubert.

The project was assigned to Schinkel in 1834 by Otto's brother and heir to the Bavarian throne, Maximilian II, who was also the brother-in-law of King Freidrich Wilhelm IV of Prussia. "I believe that any architect who is to confront the question of erecting the palace of regenerated Greece", Schinkel wrote to Maximilian, "ought first to prepare himself seriously for the task, however talented he may be as an artist. In my opinion, the choice of the site should be the first step in the creation of this work".

**36**. *K. F. Schinkel. Proposal for a royal palace on the Acropolis. Ground plan. 1834. Munich. State Drawing and Print Collection.*

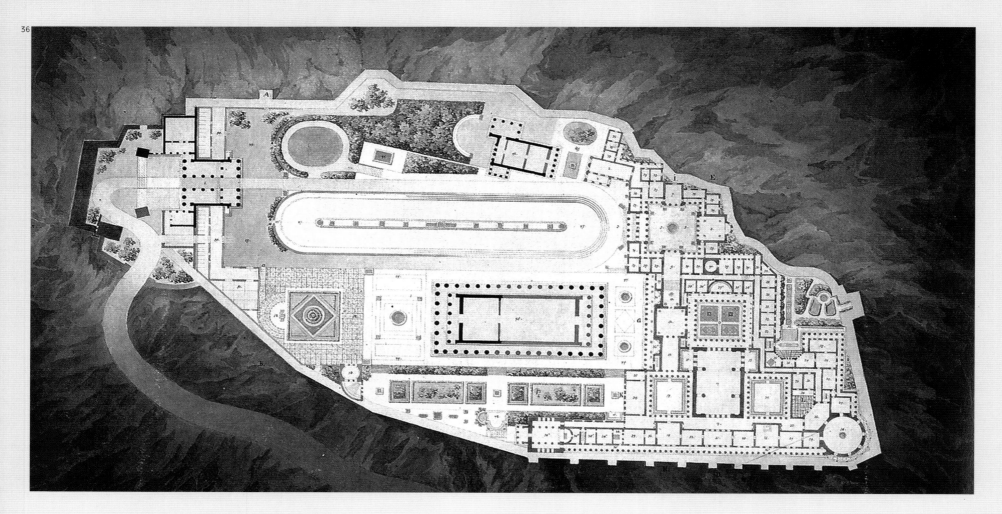

Schinkel was bold enough to take this first step. He designed the palace at Athens' very crux: on the sacred site of the Acropolis itself. It is an astonishing composition in which new and ancient buildings enter into a dialogue in a truly inventive and skilful manner. The core rooms of the palace extended over the south-east of the site. However, despite Schinkel's efforts to respect the ancient monuments, it is evident that he failed to do so in a number of instances.

Alexander Ferdinand von Quast (1807-1876), an architect and architecture historian who had studied under Schinkel and was later appointed Prussia's general inspector of antiquities, firmly believed the king should dwell once more in the ancient castle of Cecrops and build his royal chambers beside the house of Erechtheus. He describes Schinkel's plan with admiration: "The new Propylaea stand opposite the ancient Propylaea, forming a line behind the east façades of the Parthenon and the Erechtheum, and their layout is akin to that of the age of Pericles", writes Quast, before going on to describe the buildings Schinkel sited on the site. The palace itself was located behind the Parthenon and consisted of a low, free composition of volumes with courtyards and open spaces between them, porticos and a peristyle, all enhanced with greenery, flowers and orange trees. Quast proposed that the new town should be built at the foot of the rock, with the state ministries and a large square in the foreground.

**37.** *K. F. Schinkel. Proposal for a royal palace on the Acropolis. W elevation. 1834. Munich. State Drawing and Print Collection.*

Modern scholars who have studied the work of the great German architect have repeatedly analysed and investigated this project, pointing out *inter alia* its skilful adjustment to the local climate and living conditions, the discreet way in which it integrates into its environment and the masterful blending of old and new. Most of which is demonstrably accurate, though it does not answer the crucial question posed by Papageorgiou-Venetas: "Where did Schinkel find the courage to suggest this juxtaposition?" I tend to agree with Klenze, who states that "The plan was an exquisite and alluring architectural *Midsummer Night's Dream*". That is exactly how I view the "Palace on the Acropolis": as a stage set like those designed for Mozart's opera *The Magic Flute* in 1815 or Gluck's *Armide* in 1820; a stage set that inspired the generation of architects and archaeologists who visited Paris, Rome and Athens in the Grand Tour of the 19th and early 20th century and strove to produce more or less well-documented reconstructions of the Acropolis, Delphi, Olympia and other archaeological sites, putting the idiom of ancient architectural forms to playful use. Schinkel, too, was well acquainted with this game.

The proposal to erect a palace on the Acropolis was rejected outright by Ludwig himself, who dispatched Leo von Klenze, inspector of the royal buildings of the Bavarian court, head of the nation's superior building service, confidant and statue-maker to Greece in July 1834 to revise Kleanthis and Schaubert's Plan.

Still, King Otto wavered for many days before he was finally convinced that this idea, though fine, was not practical. With a sigh, he rejected the bold dream.

**38.** *K. F. Schinkel. Proposal for a royal palace on the Acropolis. The central chamber. 1834. Munich. State Drawing and Print Collection.*

**39.** *Karl Friedrich Schinkel. Proposal for a royal palace on the Acropolis. 1834. Munich. State Drawing and Print Collection.*
*a) E-W Section, looking northwards.*
*b) N-S Section, looking eastwards.*
*c) E-W Section, looking southwards.*

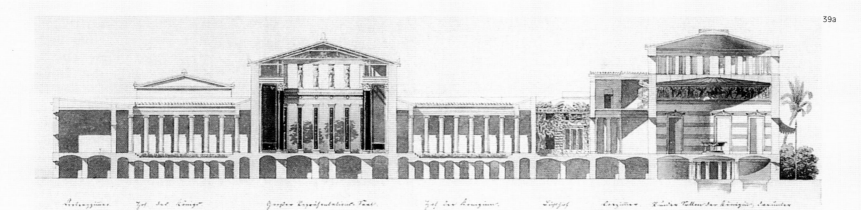

Wohnzimmer    Hof des Königs    Großer Repräsentations Saal    Hof der Königin    Lichthof    Corridor    Kleiner Vorhalle der Königin, darunter Keller

Durchschnitt des Pallastes nach der Richtung K.L.C. gegen Norden gesehen.

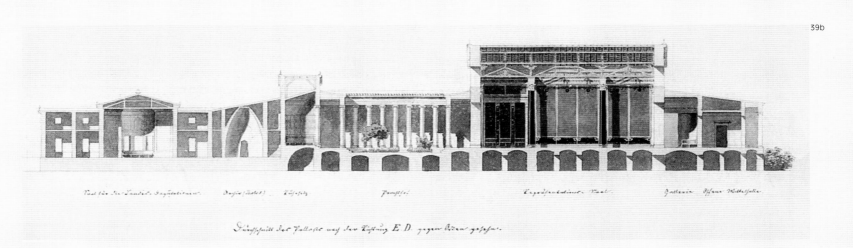

Saal für die Landes Deputationen    Bassin (Hotel)    Lichthof    Pompshof    Repräsentations Saal    Gallerie Offene Mittelhalle

Durchschnitt des Pallastes nach der Richtung E.D. gegen Osten gesehen.

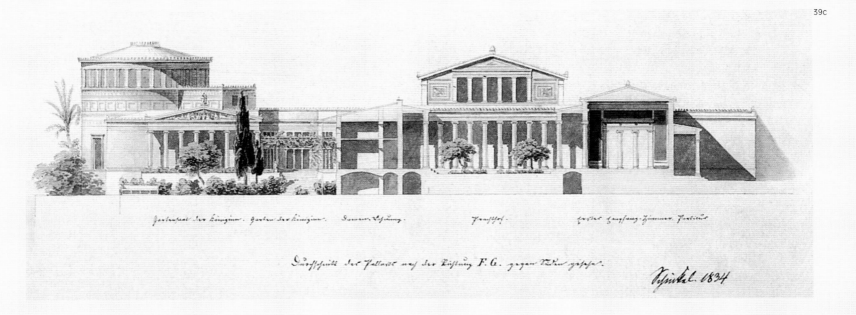

Gartensaal der Königin    Garten der Königin    Dienerwohnung    Pompshof    Großes Empfang Zimmer Portikus

Durchschnitt des Pallastes nach der Richtung F.G. gegen Westen gesehen.

Schinkel. 1834

**41**

## KLENZE'S PROPOSAL

Following the rejection of Schinkel's design, Klenze proposed that the palace be built on Agios Athanasios hill in Kerameikos and drew up plans for the project. As far as the Acropolis was concerned, Klenze noted that Schinkel's proposal would involve the demolition of all the later "barbaric" additions to the Acropolis as well as the removal of marble fragments for use in building the palace, which would leave the site uncluttered. That said, he did not hesitate to include the Theseion in his own design for the royal palace though, admittedly, it was not incorporated into the building complex itself, but rather into a large English-style garden covering a considerable part of the Theseion area and the still-unexcavated Ancient Agora. The ministries were to be built on what we now know to be the site of the ancient Kerameikos cemetery, though this had still to be located at the time.

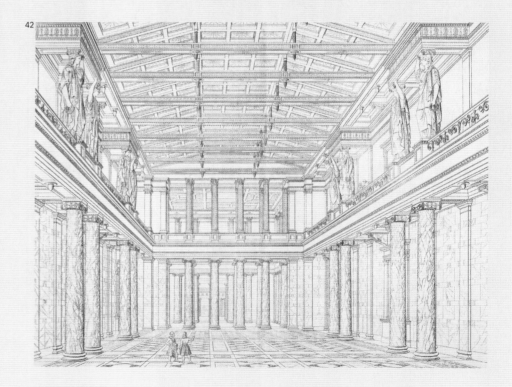

**40.** *Leo von Klenze (1784-1864).*

**41.** *Leo von Klenze. City Plan for New Athens, approved September 1834.*

**42.** *Leo von Klenze. Proposal for a royal palace on Agios Athanasios Hill, Athens. Perspective of the reception room. 1834. Lithograph. National Historical Museum.*

No complete set of drawings of Klenze's palace survives. On the basis of evidence derived from the general topographic survey of Athens, the palace was to have stood on a large flat area on the summit of the hill. Its rectangular ground plan was closed on three sides and open on the fourth facing the park. Two enclosed atria were cut into the mass of the building while a larger courtyard enclosed on three sides, as we noted, possessed an impressive south-east-facing portico.

Large flights of steps and ramps on the north-west side of the palace were to have linked it with the lower town and the state ministries. The royal stables were placed on an intermediate level facing north, while two small buildings –small prostyle temples in design, one housing Otto's Catholic chapel, the other a Lutheran chapel for Amalia's use– were connected by a portico to the royal apartments in front of the short north-west side of the complex. The semicircular belvedere terrace in front of them was to have enjoyed a view of the Acropolis. The open space between this and the palace would have featured a large statue of Pallas Athena, similar to that created by Pheidias, while a semicircular double staircase led down to the garden.

44

**43**. *Leo von Klenze. Proposal for a royal palace on Agios Athanasios Hill, Athens. Northern elevation. 1834. Munich. State Drawing and Print Collection.*

**44**. *Leo von Klenze. Wall decoration for the northern arcade in the royal gardens at Ludwig I's palace in Munich. Munich. State Drawing and Print Collection.*

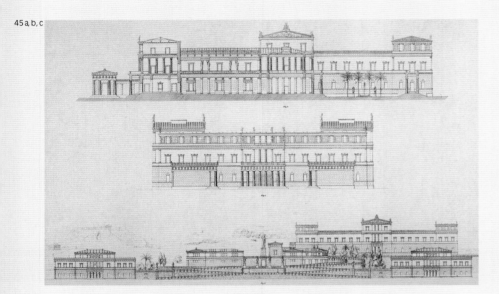

45 a, b, c

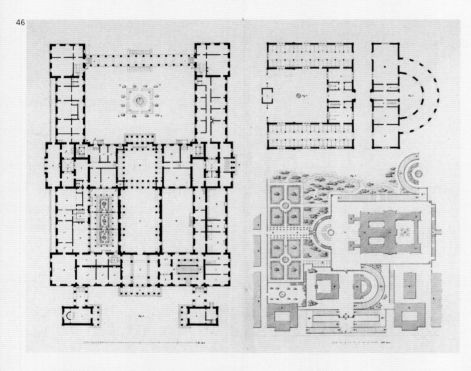

46

**45.** *The royal palace complex on Agios Athanasios Hill. Lithograph. 1838.*
*National Historical Museum.*
*a) Section, looking SE.*
*b) NE elevation.*
*c) NW elevation. A ministry is visible on the extreme left.*

The style and morphology of this large neoclassical building can be gleaned from some of Klenze's drawings preserved in the State Graphic Arts Collection in Munich, and from an excellent perspective drawing of the palace which is now in the Hermitage Museum, St Petersburg: the palace was to have two storeys with three-storey sections at the four corners of the rectangle and in the middle of the long sides at either end of the perpendicular wing. These six three-storey 'towers' project forward slightly of the rest of the building. The entire palace is covered by a flat roof, apart from the two three-storey towers on the central wing, which have tiled roofs. The main entrance is emphasised by a Doric porch whose roof serves as a balcony for the Ionic upper storey. The columns on the second-storey balcony follow the Corinthian order in accordance with the conventions of neoclassical morphology. On the crowning of this central section, the main pediment bears the royal coat-of-arms and is adorned by sculpted winged figures [Nikes] at the apex and corners. Statues also adorn the corners of the four corner towers, while metopes adorned with decorative scenes were planned for the gaps between the openings.

The ground floor was constructed out of large exposed blocks of even course-work masonry whose great height would have provided the building with a solid visual base. The first and second storeys have a plain plaster surface. The impression of solidity is strengthened further by the robust stone pedestal formed by the polygonal blocks of the supporting walls.

The sparing use of colour on the pediments, cornices, metopes, and elsewhere makes for an interesting effect.

Klenze's design is distinguished by its austerity and Classical clarity, as well as by a flexible stylistic approach that reveals his expertise and talent. Everything in the composition bears the stamp of a sagely expressed balance and reciprocity between the individual elements and the whole.

Although the south side of the building, which is enclosed by the garden, faces the Acropolis, no provision appears to have been made for any direct link between the two. Klenze's design thus forms part of a conceptual triangle whose apexes were at Othonos (now Omonoia) Square (the site of the cathedral: the church of God the Saviour of Greece), the Kerameikos and another, smaller church in what is now Syntagma, and which highlights three ideological reference points: God, ancient Greece and the King.

Klenze envisioned the palace gardens and courtyards planted with cypress, olive and palm trees – a vision he extended, it may be noted, to the Acropolis itself, since he was much taken with the idea of inserting ancient Greek sculpture and architecture amidst clumps of trees to imbue them with a picturesque quality.

Although Klenze's vision was rejected in the case of the Acropolis by its Greek conservators, it has unfortunately been implemented, either deliberately or out of negligence, in many other ancient Greek monuments, which are now either partly or completely concealed from the visitor's gaze.

**46**. *The palace complex on Agios Athanasios Hill. Lithograph. 1838. National Historical Museum. Ground plan. Bottom right: general layout of the palace complex. Note the ministries to the NW of the palace and the imposing staircase leading to the main entrance. Top right: plan of the stables and coach house.*

**47**. *Leo von Klenze. Proposal for a royal palace on Agios Athanasios Hill, Athens. View from the South. 1835. Oil painting. Saint Petersburg. Hermitage Museum.*

## LANGE'S PROPOSED PALACE

**48**. *Ludwig Lange (1806-1868).*

L udwig Lange first came to Athens in the spring of 1834 at the age of 26. He was accompanying his Techniques teacher from the University of Munich, Carl Rottmann, who had come to paint a series of Greek landscapes. These were later to be used to decorate the arcades in the gardens of Ludwig's royal palace in Bavaria, where he had just completed a similar series of murals with classical Italian landscapes. Lange was subsequently appointed to teach painting at the Athens Gymnasium for the new academic year beginning in September 1835. "The pupils at the Greek School can also attend the lesson [...]. Because it may be expected that Herr Lange's skill will help those attending his lessons to make great progress, the Secretary [of Education] is henceforth to refer all those seeking help in obtaining a place abroad to be taught Painting to the Athens Gymnasium, where they can undertake their preliminary studies, and would like to inform them that in this case alone can they apply to receive a scholarship while studying abroad, having pursued every possible avenue in that regard". As well as teaching, Lange also sought to make his name as an architect; indeed, this seems to have been his main focus, as he was often negligent with regard to his teaching duties, "claiming that hour upon hour of ceaseless tuition befuddled his senses".

It is obvious that Lange, along with the other young architects who had come to Greece, had dreams of a glorious career as an architect in a period of reconstruction. Which is how he came to draft complete plans in 1835 for both a sea-side mansion in Piraeus and a royal palace in Athens, as well as two plans for the Athens Gymnasium in 1836, the University in 1837 and the Anglican and God the Saviour churches in 1838, all of which were rejected one by one by Schaubert and the Ministry of the Interior. He had not been officially commissioned for any of them.

Disheartened and dissatisfied with teaching Painting alone, Lange requested permission to depart for Munich in April 1838 "to revive his spirit, which had grown turgid in Greece, and to form relationships with important personages in

Germany who could play a key role in the building of the Church of God the Saviour [in Athens]".

Returning to Munich, he took with him a large number of landscapes in watercolour, drawings of folk costumes etc. which are now held in Munich's State Collection of Drawings and Engravings. Lange would return to Greece in May 1839 to submit his resignation.

Lange drew up his plan for a palace in Athens in October 1835, a short while after von Klenze. As he lived in Athens, he had a more direct relationship with the city's topography and with the views held by Athenian society at the time, and was undoubtedly aware of the critical comments expressed in the Athens press, which noted that even the Turks preferred to build their homes in Boubounistra, an area in the north-east of the city, and not in the "Kletzikon area", where everyone knew the stagnant water made for unhealthy living conditions. (Indeed, until the early 20th century, when the city's Gas Works were built there, the local inhabitants continued to suffer from malaria).

**49**. *Ludwig Lange. Proposal for a palace at Athens. 1835.*
*Munich. State Drawing and Print Collection.*

49

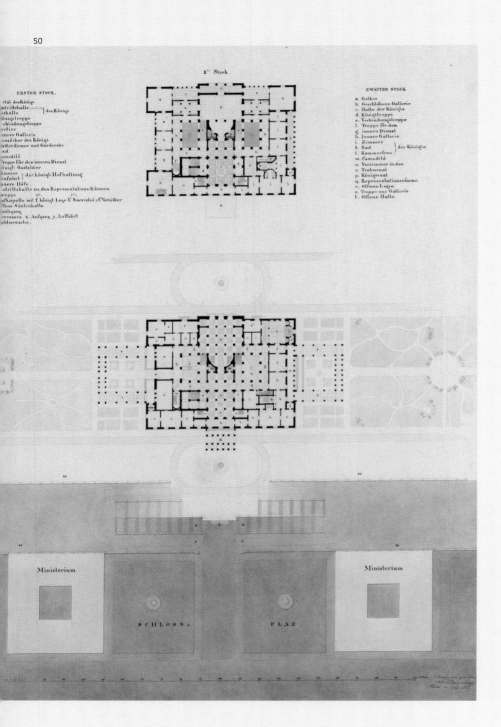

**50.** *L. Lange. Proposal for a palace at Athens. Floor plans for the ground and upper storeys. 1835. Munich. State Drawing and Print Collection.*

Lange therefore positioned his palace on the south-western slope of Lycabettus Hill (which is where the palace was finally built). The ground plan formed a closed rectangle 75 metres by 55 metres with two small internal atria measuring 10x15 metres each. The two narrow sides extended, on the ground floor, into two colonnades on each side.

According to the memorandum, the central section contained a large hall on its ground floor from which the royal staircase led up to a second large hall on the upper storey and a reception room joined by two smaller staircases to the royal chamber (ball room). The central wing was taller than the two side ones to allow the ball room to have a higher roof. According to Papageorgiou-Venetas, the central wing had a third storey (an attic?) which was to have been visible from the side but concealed by the crowning at the front. However, given the absence of a ground or cross-sectional plan, the existence of an attic cannot be proved (personally, however, I consider it unlikely that the architect envisioned an attic over the royal chamber). The right wing housed the queen's chambers and the royal chapel, with the king's apartments on the upper storey. The ground floor of the left wing was given over to the offices of the adjutants, secretaries etc., the upper storey to the throne room and a number of salons and reception rooms whose confused arrangement reveals either rushed preparation or the youthful Lange's inexperience.

The building had a flat roof, except for the central section which had a hipped roof. The articulation of the façades is also indicative of Lange's inexperience.

The main frontage is austere and heavy. With its Doric central entrance, matching pair of circular staircases and a ramp for carriages, it closely follows the models contained in the architectural manuals of the day. A quad at a lower level was to have been flanked by the ministries of state.

The rear elevation, which faced Lycabettus Hill, aspired –unsuccessfully– to a lighter, less austere effect by means of a high central balcony the architect describes as an 'open loggia' with two Ionic columns supporting an impressive pediment and opening onto the 'royal chamber'. Two broader balconies (loggias) flanking it give onto four more reception rooms in their turn which inter-connect with the central chamber.

A final roofed balcony was to have been included at the rear of the king's apart-ments, directly above the gallery in front of the queen's suite.

Like Gärtner's plans, which will be examined below, Lange's design, though shar-ing a number of features with von Klenze's, is far simpler and closer to the mod-els being taught in the architectural schools of the day. Although many argue that both Lange and Gärtner had copied von Klenze, I believe the similarities be-tween their designs are largely the result of a shared approach and of the mod-els of the era.

Ultimately, Klenze's palace stands out not so much for its size (at 13,524 sq.m. including the grounds, it was roughly twice as large as Lange's and Gärtner's proposals) as for its monumental and integrated architectural conception.

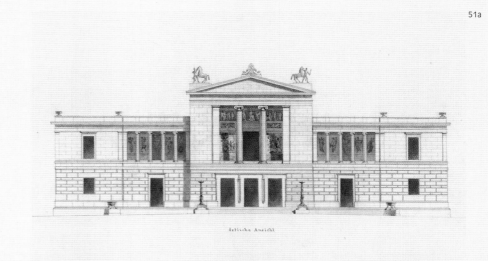

51. *L. Lange. Proposal for a palace at Athens. a. Front elevation, b. Side elevation. 1835. Munich. State Drawing and Print Collection.*

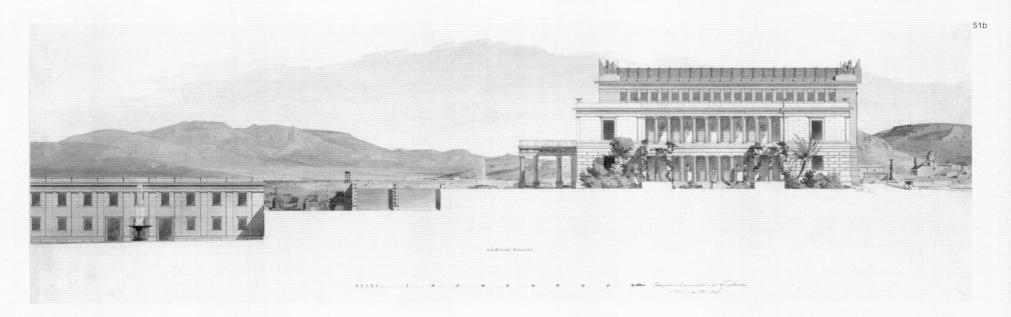

# GÄRTNER'S PALACE
## (THE HELLENIC PARLIAMENT BUILDING)

**N**either Klenze's nor Lange's designs were destined to be implemented. As we have seen, Klenze had fallen into disfavour shortly after his return from Greece and Ludwig would henceforth promote his main rival, F. Gärtner. Klenze's arrogance and thirst for power irritated Ludwig, who often said "I don't have favourites, in art or in politics". Gärtner's time had come.

Friedrich Gärtner was the son of the court architect, Andrew Gärtner, whom Klenze had successfully displaced in 1816 when he renewed his youthful friendship with Ludwig. Having studied in Munich and then Paris, like any self-respecting architect he visited Rome and the Bay of Naples, where the antiquities of Pompeii and Herculaneum, which had come to light only a few years earlier, were a magnet for the architects of the day. Having returned to Munich in 1817, he was appointed to a teaching post at the Academy a few years later and won the favour of Ludwig, who began to promote him systematically at Klenze's expense.

*52. Friedrich von Gärtner (1791-1847).*

*53. Friedrich von Gärtner at work in Athens. 1836. Munich Polytechnic Architecture Museum.*

*54. The royal stables with the palace in the background. Lithograph. Royal Printing Press. Private collection.*

*55. F. Altenhoven. Athens City Plan with the palace on the site where it was actually built, in Syntagma Square. 1837.*

**Pages 52-53**
*56. Friedrich von Gärtner. The Athens Palace. Front elevation. National Historical Museum.*

*57. The Athens Palace. View from Syntagma Square.*

*58. The Athens Palace (Hellenic Parliament). View from the Tomb of the Unknown Soldier.*

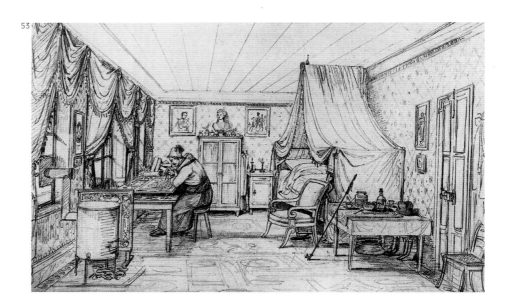

When, in 1835, Ludwig finally fulfilled the dream of visiting Greece he had nurtured since his youth, he was accompanied not by Klenze, who had already returned to Munich in the autumn of 1834, but by Gärtner. The trip was a success: "I shall fly on the winds, I shall cleave the air, I am flooded with unprecedented joy," the architect wrote on returning from his enchanting journey.

On his visit, Klenze had been charged with checking and revising the Athens town plan drawn up by Kleanthis and Schaubert and, secondarily, with selecting a site for Otto's palace. Klenze's modifications to the town plan seem to have been carried out solely because changes had to be made. Perhaps the Bavarian royal court's inspector of buildings took a somewhat jaundiced view of the rise of two young architects, both Schinkel's students Kleanthis and Schaubert, the latter already assigned to a senior public position as director of town plans and buildings at the Ministry of Internal Affairs. Indeed, though there is no evidence to support this, it is said they had already sent a copy to their teacher to solicit his opinion. Klenze's decision to move the site of the palace to the Kerameikos thus appears to be nothing more than change for the sake of change.

When Ludwig arrived in Athens with his new favourite, the question of the location of the palace was still unresolved. In early December 1835, Gärtner and Otto toured the city to inspect all the proposed sites and, although Otto was still much taken with Schinkel's idea, it was ultimately decided to build the palace on the hill above what is now Syntagma Square – a site recommended by Dr Roser and Dr Wibmer, the royal physicians, as being the healthiest.

Its location close to the old town certainly satisfied many native Athenians. At the same time, land expropriation began in the area and was to continue over the following decades with the later aim of creating the royal gardens, Syntagma Square and of building "public offices for the Ministries and the Council of State" on Kifissias (now Vasilissis Sophias) Avenue, though this was never done, since the state was never able to amass the funds required.

Gärtner made his preliminary drawings in situ with extreme rapidity over the first months of 1836. It was only then, in March 1836, that Schinkel learned that his

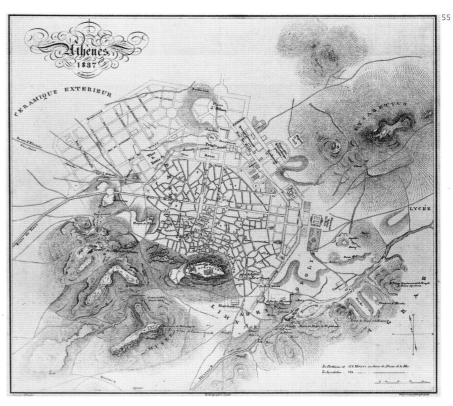

59

**59.** *The Athens Palace. View of the side entrance (latter half of the 19th century).*

**60.** *The Athens Palace (Hellenic Parliament). View of the side entrance today.*

plan was not to be implemented. On 28 March 1836, the writer, Prince Hermann von Pückler-Muskau –prince of Bad Muskau in Saxony– who was in Athens at this time, informed him that his proposal had been rejected:

"My dear friend", he wrote, "I have been informed that you have been given no news or any token of recognition or gratitude, indeed, not so much as a simple response, to your superb design, which is pure poetry and beauty [...]. Instead of sending you an answer, they have forgotten you. You have not been forgotten, however, by the new king, who is enthused both by your person and your idea. It was the first thing he mentioned to me, and the following day he sent Gärtner to me with your design, which he looks upon as the ideal against which to compare the prosaic project that is to be implemented. It is not the new king that will decide, however. The die is cast".

Following his departure from Greece at the end of March and his return to Munich in April of the same year, Gärtner continued to work on the project intensively in 1843. His archive, which is now held in the Munich Technical University Architecture Museum, contains two hundred and forty-seven drawings of architectural and structural designs and proposals for the interior decorations of the palace rooms.

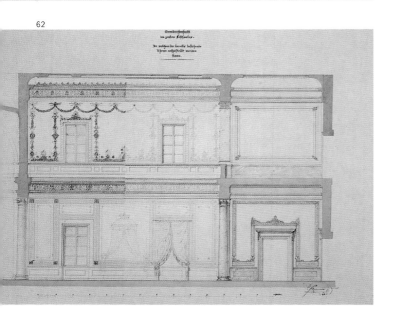

Plafond des Durchganges der beiden Logen.

Plafond des großen Festsaals, in welchem der Thron auf- gestellt werden kann.

**61.** *Friedrich von Gärtner. The Athens Palace. Ball room section. 1842. Munich Polytechnic Architecture Museum.*

**62.** *Friedrich von Gärtner. The Athens Palace. Main reception room section. 1844. Munich Polytechnic Architecture Museum.*

**63.** *Friedrich von Gärtner. The Athens Palace. Study for the painted decoration on the ceilings in the reception room. Munich Polytechnic Architecture Museum.*

**64.** *The Athens Palace (Hellenic Parliament). The Trophy room with the frieze depicting episodes from Modern Greek history by L. Schwanthaler.*

65. *Friedrich von Gärtner. The Athens Palace. Study for the painted decoration in the Audience Room. Munich Polytechnic Architecture Museum.*

66. *Friedrich von Gärtner. The Athens Palace. Study for a wall decoration. Munich Polytechnic Architecture Museum.*

Although Gärtner's design does have much in common with Klenze's proposal, it is certainly no imitation. Similar designs, as we have seen, are to be found in the manual written by Jean-Nicolas-Louis Durand, who was appointed to a teaching post at the Munich Academy in 1895, and in other architectural handbooks of its kind.

Indeed, Durand's handbook contains at least two ground plans, accompanied by corresponding façades, that could be regarded as both reference and starting points for Klenze and Gärtner's proposed palace complexes. The same handbook also illustrates types of building façades that might be regarded as the starting points for large building projects Gärtner designed in Munich.

"When we observe monuments and consider their cause", Durand writes in his introduction, "it is evident that architecture's object was never to be pleasing". He goes on to add: "The size, majesty, splendour, luxury, variety, impression and character one discerns in buildings are undoubtedly important factors in their beauty and the satisfaction one feels when one is faced with them. But is there a need to pursue these, given that one has a building that serves the use for which it is intended in a fitting manner? No, the architect should concern himself with function alone". Gärtner's architecture would thus seem to follow these basic principles, which are to be found in the work of several other contemporary architects, at least in part.

The palace building Gärtner designed for Otto was an austere, frugal, neoclassical edifice not because funds were not available for a more opulent or grandiose building, but because austerity and frugality were the keynotes of Gärtner's architectural approach. The first designs (no copies of which have ever, unfortunately, come to light) produced by him in his atelier in Athens was probably more representative of this approach, but they were rejected by Ludwig, who was a difficult and autocratic employer and had no qualms about drawing a line through anything that offended him. Commenting on the final result, the architect was moved to observe: "All that's left is a military camp".

Inside the building, however, Gärtner took his revenge, as we shall see. As early as 1816, he had visited southern Italy and been captivated by Pompeii and its wall-paintings. In the spring of 1839, he returned to Rome and Pompeii to make scale drawings, and it was with these impressions still fresh in his mind that he designed the wall-paintings for the royal palace in Athens. When he quit Athens, he left behind his pupil, Johann Ernst Eduard Riedel, an architect and landscape gardener, to supervise the completion of the work. As court architect, Riedel settled in Athens with his young wife and undertook freelance commissions in addition to supervising work on the palace. According to Christiana Lutt, the

67. *Friedrich von Gärtner. The Athens Palace. Study for the wall and ceiling decoration in the Games room. 1843. Munich Polytechnic Architecture Museum.*

68. *Friedrich von Gärtner. The Athens Palace. Study for the d cor in the King's study. Munich Polytechnic Architecture Museum.*

69. *Friedrich von Gärtner. The Athens Palace. Study for the painted decoration in the Queen's bedroom. Munich Polytechnic Architecture Museum.*

70. *The Athens Palace. Main entrance (photograph from the latter half of the 19th century).*

71. *The Athens Palace (Hellenic Parliament). View from the Royal (National) Gardens.*

72, 73. *Friedrich von Gärtner. The Athens Palace. Details of acroteria on pediments. Munich Polytechnic Architecture Museum.*

74. *The Athens Palace (Hellenic Parliament). The rear entrance.*

wife of Amalia's chaplain, Riedel was envious of the Hansen brothers, whom the king thought highly of, and was afraid that one of them would be preferred over him. As Riedel realised, despite his inflated sense of self-esteem, the Hansens were both more intelligent and more capable than he was. If Gärtner had designed the building as he did because of financial constraints, he would never have included the lavish interior decoration which took a full eight years to complete (1840-1848).

The palace was certainly a heavy building. The criticism levelled at it by foreign visitors to Athens seems to have been of considerable concern to the royal family itself. In a file in the Otto Archive in the Greek State Archives (inv. no. 333), there is a hand-written copy of an unidentified document that describes the palace thus:

"The new king's palace stands on the edge of the city's main thoroughfare and also at its end – for the present, at least, since the city is extending very rapidly. The street is very beautiful; but location-wise, I can find nothing to praise about the architecture or the construction of the royal palace. The building lacks so much as a single fine room, while the reception rooms give onto dark internal courtyards instead of the beautiful views which the building's location has secured for it. There are three chapels at three corners of the building [this information must be mistaken]: one for the Catholics, to serve the king, one Protestant for the queen, and a Greek church for their children who, it has been agreed, will subscribe to the Orthodox faith. For the present, though, there are still no signs of pregnancy after four years of marriage, while the crown is debarred from passing on to his brother, since it has been specifically agreed that the crowns of Bavaria and Greece cannot sit upon the same head.

The palace's columns, pilasters and window-frames are of the finest marble, but the latter are all of the same small size and set in a straight line along the façade, giving the impression of a barracks or a hospital.

It is true that there is a colonnade, but this is low, small and devoid of interest. The royal walls are built, strange as it may seem, of exposed masonry, like garden walls, and the workmanship is not particularly meticulous, while the con-

75

75. TThe Athens Palace (Hellenic Parliament). Detail of the rear pediment.

76. The Athens Palace (Hellenic Parliament). View of the southern arcade looking towards the garden.

Pages 66-67
77. The Athens Palace (Hellenic Parliament). South elevation.

trast between the dressed-stone cornices and the rest of the courtyard with its rubble masonry is utterly lamentable. Despite this, it is said that the palace, even as it is, has already cost thousands of Pounds and that it will take another 6,000 to finish it; where the money will be found to pay for what has already been done, far less for the expenses that are still required to finish it, is anyone's guess [...]. Bavarian sculptors, painters, etc. etc. have descended in swarms from Munich to work on this building. This is the Palace of Athens".

This highly critical commentary was probably written in 1840, four years after Otto's marriage to Amalia, meaning that the writer did not have the finished building before him.

In November 1840, when building work was completed, Gärtner returned to Athens with a team of six architects, three painters specialising in historical subjects and an interior decorator with ten assistants. The architects were his son, Friedrich Gärtner, his nephew Karl Friedrich Andreas Klumpp, Friedrich Buerklein, Eduard Riedel, Franz Beyschlag and Langenmantel; the three painters were Claudius von Schraudolph, Ulrich Halbreiter and Joseph Kranzenberger; while the team of decorators and painters was led by J. Schwarmann. A second group of experienced artists came to Greece to paint the great frieze in the Trophy Room designed by the sculptor Ludwig Michael von Schwanthalez. This frieze contained depictions of the most important events in the struggle for Greek Independence including the swearing of the oath at Vostitsa, Otto's arrival in Naf-plion, the national assembly at Kalamata, the murder of Patriarch Gregory, symbolic depictions of Greek victories on land and at sea, the national assembly at Epidaurus, the destruction of Messolongi, the Treaty of London and the founding of the Panhellenion by Ioannis Kapodistrias.

Thirteen portraits hung in the Trophy and adjutants' rooms set in round frames: twelve of Greek freedom fighters and one of the philhellene, F.A. Hastings. These two rooms and the grand staircase are the only elements of the original interior decoration that have survived, conserved or reconstructed, to this day. For eight years, the palace was a huge studio full of German, Italian and Greek artists toiling to create a residence worthy of a king.

78. *The Athens Palace (Hellenic Parliament). Auxiliary entrance.*

79. *The Athens Palace (Hellenic Parliament). Lamp column on the western elevation.*

Inside the building –a solid closed rectangular structure with a central wing– the distribution of functions mirrors the austere logic that informs the façades. The two large internal courtyards created on either side of the central block were never intended to be large internal atria with colonnades, like true courtyards, in which the life of the inhabitants could be extended out into the open air, but simply to serve as two large light-wells for the corridors, staircases and ancillary rooms. By placing storerooms and toilets facing onto the courtyards on the ground floor instead of workrooms, Gärtner manages to invalidate the rationale of the courtyard as this had been understood throughout the ancient Greek and Roman world and survived into the first years after Liberation in the form of the Athenian house. Indeed, a link through open or semi-open spaces with the open air –which was so essential in view of the Greek climate, and which Schinkel and Klenze had integrated so sensitively into their palace designs– does not seem to have concerned Gärtner in the slightest. In fact, the building has just three balconies: one above the entrance porch on the first floor of the central wing, from which the King could appear to address the crowds on official occasions, a smaller one set above the porch at the eastern entrance and a long balcony running the entire length of the south wing where the king's private apartments were located. Despite the wonderful view it affords of the Acropolis, the Saronic gulf, Mount Hymettus and later the royal gardens, even this balcony seems simply to be the unplanned consequence of the long portico beneath it; indeed, being very long (50 m.) and narrow (2.5 m.), the balcony is not a pleasant place to spend one's time. That Gärtner did not consider the possibility of the balcony being used is clear, too, from the fact that of all the rooms facing on to it only one actually communicates with it through a French window, and this was the Queen's dressing room rather than a sitting room. On the ground floor, too, the portico communicated with the palace interior via a vestibule leading to a central staircase. Of the pair of staircases at the end of the south wing, the eastern one was due to reasons of symmetry and led to a blank wall (the sanctuary of Otto's chapel); the western staircase led directly into a large sitting room which was known as the "garden room", since Gärtner had planned a small

80. *The Athens Palace. The Adjutants' room in a lithograph by Sotiris Christidis from an oil painting of 1847.*
*Royal Printing Press. Museum of the City of Athens.*

81. *The Athens Palace (Hellenic Parliament). The Adjutants' room.*

82

82. *The Athens Palace. Detail of a wall-painting in the Trophy room depicting Ludwig I presenting Otto to the Greek delegation in Munich.*

83. *The Athens Palace. Detail of a wall-painting in the Trophy room depicting Otto arriving in Nafplio.*

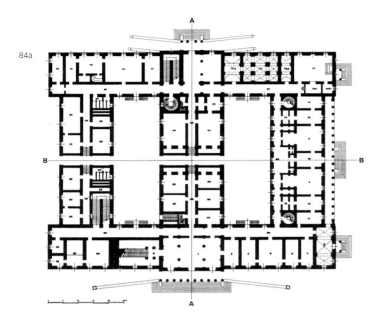

84a

flower garden on this side of the building in his original drawings. The rooms, as described by Gärtner himself in notes accompanying his drawings, were arranged as follows:

The central exterior staircase on the west side with its 10-column Doric porch led to the main entrance of the palace and from there to a large hallway with administrative services to the left and a large staircase leading to the first-floor reception rooms on the right. The south wing faced the garden and housed the adjutants' quarters (bedrooms, sitting rooms and the requisite toilets). A long corridor along the side of the internal courtyard permitted communication between the west, south and north wings. The ground floor and mezzanine of the central wing were given over to ancillary rooms (kitchens, patisserie, store-rooms, etc.) and residences for the palace staff, as was the entire north wing and parts of the ground and first floors of the east wing.

The royal family's private quarters were located on the first and second floors of the east wing and the south-east part of the east wing. They communicated

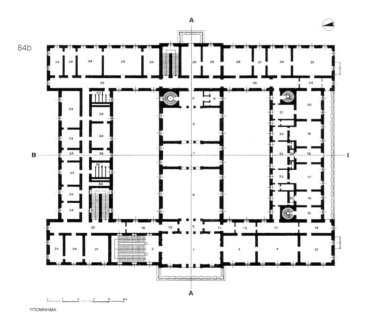

84b

ΥΠΟΜΝΗΜΑ

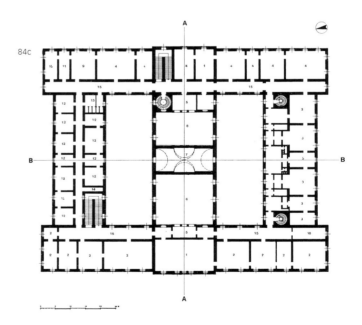

84c

84. *The Athens Palace. Plans for a) the ground floor, b) the first storey, c) the second storey. (From Aikaterini Demenegi-Viriraki, Athens' old palaces, 1836-1986).*

85. *The Athens Palace (Hellenic Parliament). Eastern elevation.*

86. *The Athens Palace (Hellenic Parliament). The main staircase (detail).*

87. *The Athens Palace (Hellenic Parliament). The main staircase.*

between themselves as well as with the adjutants' quarters by means of two small spiral staircases.

The Lord Chamberlain's quarters were located above the royal quarters in the south-east part of the east wing, with the Catholic chapel attended by Otto —which could be converted when necessary into a Protestant chapel in which Amalia could also discharge her religious duties— directly underneath on the ground floor. Later, during the reign of George I, the chapel was converted permanently for the Protestant faith, while an Orthodox chapel was created for Olga on the second floor.

The official reception rooms were in the central wing, whose ceilings were twice the height of elsewhere in the building, and in the southern part of the west wing. A large reception room (Trophy Room) stood directly opposite the central staircase, followed by the adjutants' room, the throne room and the king's study.

Gärtner designed the sculpted ceiling and wall decorations for almost all the rooms himself, along with the door and window frames, the plaster mouldings, ceiling paintings, floors (marble and high quality parquet laid out in geometrical patters), even the door handles and key plates. The German architect truly surpassed himself in his detailed designs for the walls and ceilings of the reception, throne, ball, games and dining rooms as well as for the king and queen's apartments, where the influence of his recent visit to Pompeii was most marked. All those lucky enough to have visited these rooms proffer enthusiastic descriptions.

"Most of the rooms are painted in a Pompeian style", writes Hans Christian Andersen in his book *A Journey to Greece*, "but the queen's bedroom is even stranger. It depicts an entire room full of vegetation with the blue, star-bedecked sky visible beyond the tendrils".

Most of the furnishings (the furniture, mirrors, carpets, curtains, chandeliers, candlesticks, lamps and heaters) were ordered in France at a cost of 350,000 drachmas. The most expensively furnished room in the palace was Amalia's

88

88. *The Athens Palace (Hellenic Parliament). Sculpture added at a later date to the southern elevation.*

89. *The Athens Palace (Hellenic Parliament). The ramp up to the main entrance.*

audience room, whose fittings alone cost almost 50,000 Drachmas. The total cost of building the palace is reckoned to have reached 5,240,000 Drachmas, while its final cost along with its furnishings must have approached or even surpassed 6,000,000 Drachmas, a vast sum for Greece at this time and far beyond its budget when an average bourgeois residence cost around 9,000 Drachmas to build.

In the summer of 1843, before the interior was quite complete, Otto and Amalia gave an official dinner to which, as was customary, they invited the country's political, military and religious leaders, Athens' mayor and garrison-commander, the diplomatic corps, the heads of the University and the Technical University, the headmaster of the Gymnasium, courtiers, freedom fighters and their families and the members of Athenian high society. After the dinner, the royal couple gave their guests a guided tour of the building.

The flaunting of all this wealth and luxury may have played a part in hastening the uprising of the Third of September a few months later. From the large balcony on the palace's western façade, Otto told the Greek people he was granting them the constitution they so greatly desired, and that the square in front of the palace was henceforth to be named Constitution [Syntagma] Square, a name it still bears. Although Otto contemplated abdication for several days, his *amour propre* prevailed in the end; only three weeks later, he named Dimitris Kallergis his adjutant at a new reception in the palace.

While work on the palace was still in progress, the royal balls were held in the west wing. On New Year's day 1848, the grand staircase was inaugurated with the royal couple formally descending it to attend the New Year's Day doxology. The bishop of Attica, who blessed the new staircase, compared it to a staircase to heaven with angels ascending and descending.

Finally, late in 1848, the three large reception rooms, the ballroom, the games room and the dining room in the central wing were all officially opened. The rooms were connected with each other and with the vestibules of the west and east wings through six-metre wide central openings. All the rooms were lavishly

and majestically decorated, and both the ballroom and the dining room contained a small dais for an orchestra.

Balls usually began at around nine in the evening and lasted late into the night, ending at three in the morning. The ballroom was empty apart from a row of seats along both sides and the king and queen's thrones on the left. Amalia, who had a weakness for clothes, is said to have requested that ladies should not appear in the palace wearing the same gown on more than one occasion; this must have created problems for several families.

On 30 December 1848, Amalia wrote to her father-in-law: "A few days ago, we held the inauguration ceremony for the great rooms which are so fine and well-proportioned that I am sorry poor Gärtner did not live to see his work complete. These three rooms, divided, as they are, by columns alone, are truly superb, as are the staircase and the porch. All the guests were dazzled".

The palace was now finished, and would provide a home for the royal couple and their staff (a state within a state of courtiers, officers and servants numbering over 450 people) for the next two decades. However, even complete, the palace did not cease to attract severe criticism.

90. *The Athens Palace (Hellenic Parliament). Detail of the northern entrance.*

91. *The Athens Palace (Hellenic Parliament). Main staircase. View from the ground floor to the first landing.*

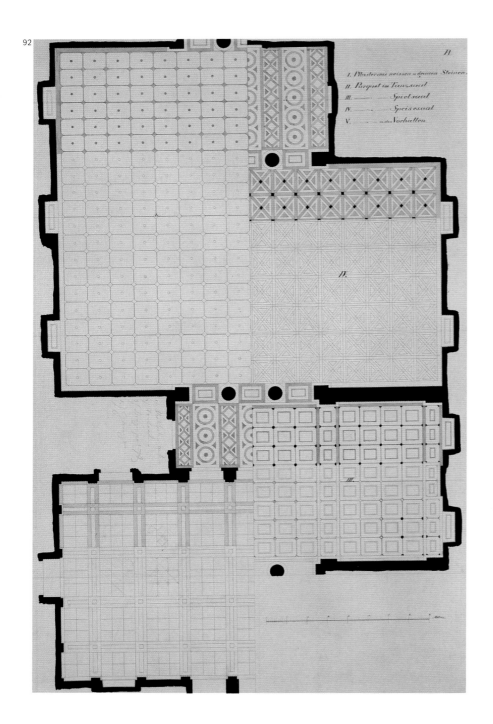

92

I.
1. *Pflasterung weissen u. grauen Steinen.*
II. *Parquet in Tanzsaal.*
III. _____ *Spielsaal.*
IV. _____ *Speisesaal.*
V. *in den Vorhallen.*

II.

III.

**92**. *Friedrich von Gärtner. The Athens Palace. Floor design for the ball room and its antechamber, the games room, the dining room and its antechamber. Munich Polytechnic Architecture Museum.*

**93**. *Friedrich von Gärtner. The Athens Palace. Door handle and lock details. Munich Polytechnic Architecture Museum.*

**94**. *Guests leaving the palace after the Hand-Kissing Ceremony. Coloured woodcut. 1889. Private collection.*

**95**. *The Athens Palace. Throne room. Contemporary photograph.*

**96**. *Otto's throne. National Historical Museum.*

93

94

95

96

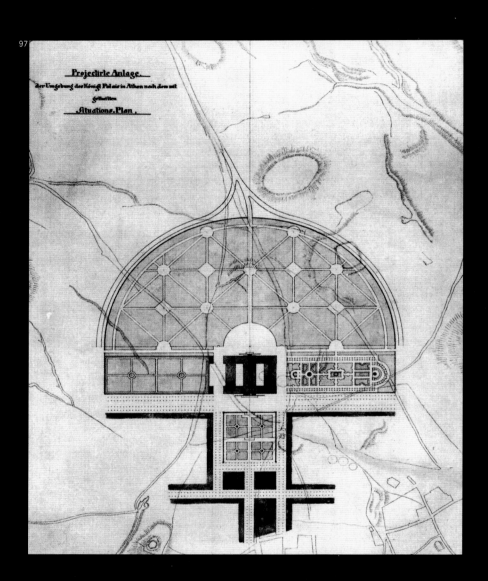

Projectirte Anlage.

der Umgebung des König. Palais in Athen nach dem seit

Situations. Plan.

**97.** *Friedrich von Gärtner. Proposal for the royal gardens and the area around the palace. 1836. Munich Polytechnic Architecture Museum.*

**98.** *Proposal for the Athens Palace, the garden of the Muses and Syntagma square. Design by the French Mission. 1889. National Historical Museum.*

Pages 86-87
**99.** *Section from the Athens City Plan (known as the "Plan Hoch") depicting the palace and the surrounding area. 1837. Benaki Museum, Neohellenic Architecture Archive.*

# THE ROYAL (NATIONAL) GARDENS

Gärtner, unlike Schinkel and Klenze, does not appear to have concerned himself with the area around the building or the garden in his initial drawings for the palace. A Secretariat of Internal Affairs memo from 1837 informs us that the government was setting aside some 50 hectares until a final decision could be taken on the exact size of the area required for the palace gardens and the ministries to be built along its north side. In a sketch dated 1836, Gärtner drew a plain semicircular garden behind the palace with decorative flower beds on either side, a flower garden to the south overlooked by the portico and the second-storey balcony, and a fruit garden to the north. In the years that followed, however, a wonderful garden covering some 15.5 hectares was created to the east and south of the palace on the initiative of Amalia, who also chose the location. The Royal (now National) Gardens are undoubtedly Amalia's personal achievement. The richest and most beautiful gardens in the capital, they took the form of a densely-planted, freely-designed garden that loosely imitated the natural landscape.

From the outset, it was designed to serve the needs of a palace garden, a public park and a botanical garden, and a committee was formed chaired by Nikolaus Karl Frass, professor of Botany at Athens University, to oversee its creation. Amalia built the gardens up at a slow and steady pace, following the dictum of her father-in-law ("I plant before I build") with whom she corresponded and whom she frequently consulted. The first steps in its design consisted of adding to the soil, digging artesian wells and repairing the old Tsakoumakos aqueduct to irrigate the garden. "The queen's garden is soaking up our water", complained the newspapers of the day; "It's guzzling it down", shouted the inhabitants of Athens, a city with a serious water shortage, but Amalia persisted: "Athens needs shade, lots of shade", Ludwig wrote to her. However, the attempts made to find water for the garden often dovetailed with efforts to solve the problems which made water such a precious commodity in the capital. The municipality called in foreign experts: in a memo on the problem to the

# AMÉNAGEMENT
## DE LA PLACE DU PALAIS ROYAL, DU JARDIN DES MUSES ET DE LA PLACE DE LA CONSTITUTION

ÉCHELLE 1:500

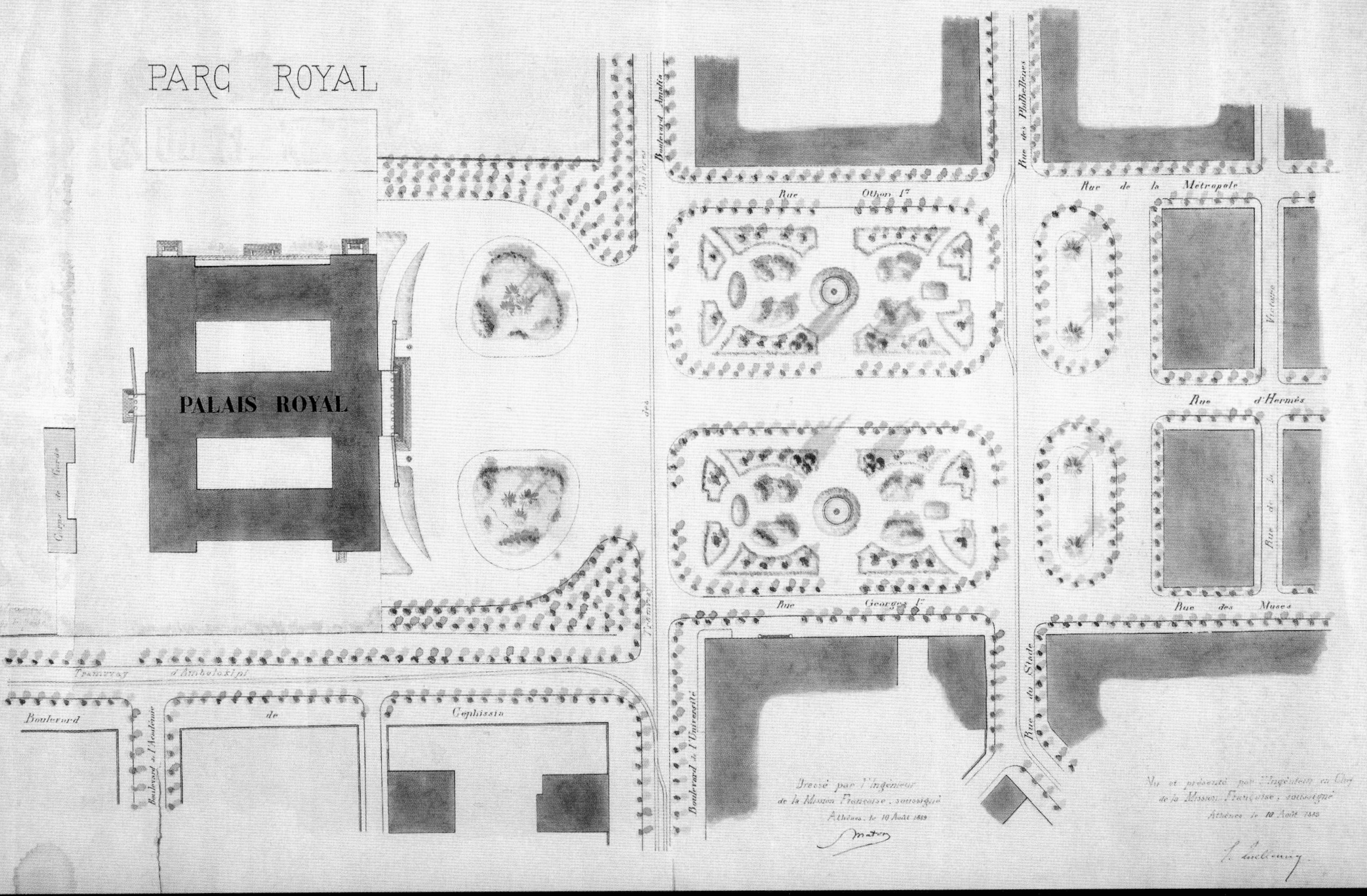

PARC ROYAL

PALAIS ROYAL

Rue Othon 1er

Rue de la Métropole

Rue d'Hermès

Rue Georges Ier

Rue des Muses

KÖNIGL. PALA

Boulevard

Hofstall

Stadion-Strasse

altes Palais

Gegenwaertiger Plan wird hiemit genehmigt.

Otto

22773.

# PLAN
### der
## Umgebung des neuen Palais

*Nota.* Die Straßen mit ☉ bezeichnet, können auch wegbleiben, und zu den vier Abtheilungen nur zwei größere gebildet werden.

Dürfte zwischen D & E müßte auf die Bauplätze Rücksicht genommen werden, so würde die roth punktirte Baulinie wegen der Symmetrie vorzuziehen seyn.

Athen den 7. Mai 1837

Koch
Ing.

Jupiter Tempel!

**100, 101.** *The Royal Gardens, late 19th and early 20th century. Postcards.*

Ανακτορικός Κήπος — Athens the garden

Athènes, Jardin Royal    Βασιλικὸς Κῆπος

**102, 103**. *The Royal Gardens, late 19th and early 20th century. Postcards.*

king, F. Boulanger mentions Souvage, who visited Athens on Kolettis' invitation in 1845, as well as the attempts made to repair the old Roman aqueducts. During the course of the digging work, fragments of ancient sculptures, the remains of an ancient building and a cistern came to light, most of which were incorporated into the design in the manner of an English garden.

We do not know who drafted the first designs for the garden, which was gradually extended between 1836 and 1859, though we do know that the German agronomist Smarat assumed initial responsibility for the project and travelled to Athens from Munich to do so. Smarat probably collaborated on the project with Riedel, who was an expert garden designer.

In her diary entry for 19 February 1848, Christiana Lutt writes: "Riedel is very busy designing the garden extension which, they say, will include the Temple of Zeus [this is confirmed by a memorandum penned by Friedrich Schmidt in 1858]. But that just isn't right! Those ruins are national monuments and nothing should be done to cut the world off from these historical memories at a time when the royal gardens are not open to everyone. This is my opinion, though nobody has ever been consulted and all the courtiers believe the king has the right to do what he wants. I, too, grant him permission to create gardens, but he should not keep the rest of us out of them". However, the young Danish woman's wish, which she expressed so passionately and with such humour, would not come to pass for several years. For the time being, Riedel seems to have been in constant conflict with the French landscape gardener, François Luis Bareaud, who had assumed responsibility for tending to the garden along with Friedrich Smith. A superb lithograph in the Otto Museum in Ottobrunn (a suburb of Munich), accurately reproduces the royal gardens as they were c.1850. According to Papageorgiou-Venetas, this design, which is entitled "Plan du Jardin Royal à Athènes" and bears neither date nor signature, must be the work of Bareaud (a similar lithograph of the Queen's Tower also has a French annotation and title and is referred to everywhere, even in German texts, as the "Tour de la Reine"), but we lack confirmation that it was designed by Bareaud along with any proof to the contrary. However, whoever the designer or designers were, the royal gardens were undoubtedly, as we have seen, the creation of the queen herself, who continued to stay abreast of the latest developments and to show an interest in the gardens even after she was deposed.

104. *The Royal Gardens. General View with the Temple of Olympian Zeus in the background. (From Marinos Vrettos, La nouvelle Athènes, 1860).*

105. *The Royal (National) Gardens.*

106. *The Royal (National) Gardens. The row of washingtonias and the sundial at the western entrance.*

107. *The Royal (National) Gardens. The artificial cave which was created and adorned with fossil crystals from Karystos.*

108. *The Royal (National) Gardens. An iron pergola covers the pond dug in the gardens' early years.*

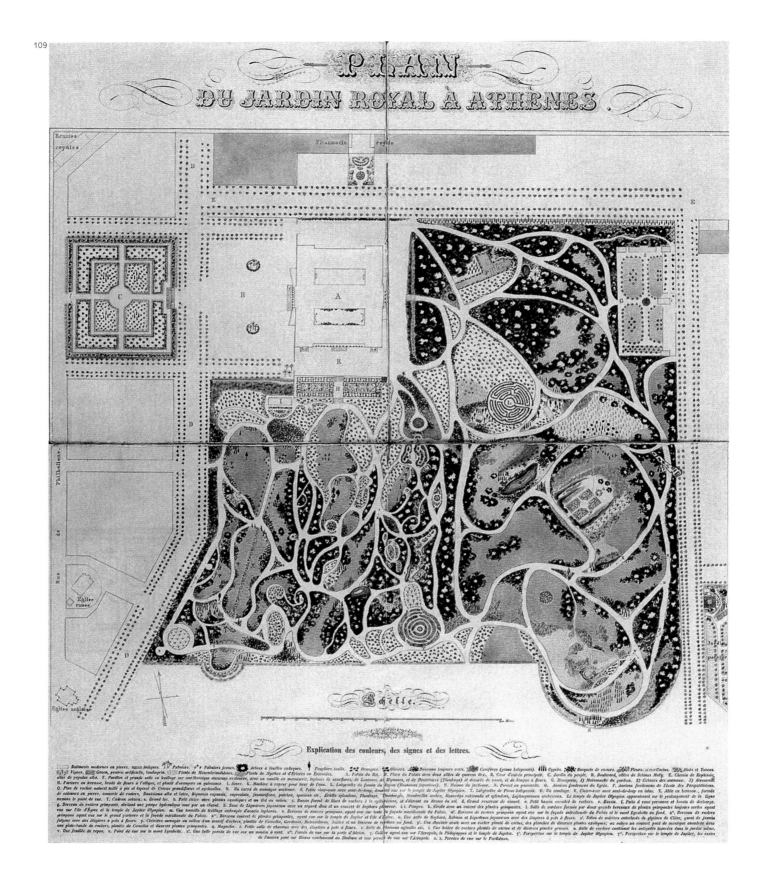

**109.** *The Royal Gardens. Ground plan (possibly by Bareaud and dating from the mid 19th century). Ottobrunn. Otto Museum.*

**110.** *The Athens Palace (Hellenic Parliament). The flight of steps descending from the southern side to the garden.*

111. *King George shortly after his arrival in Greece.*

112. *Queen Olga in her youth.*

## THE PALACE DURING THE REIGN OF GEORGE I AND AFTER IT

n Friday 24 May 1863, the Danish palace issued the following announcement: "Tomorrow, Saturday, at 12 noon, H.M. the King will be pleased to give an official audience in the palace at Christiansborg to the committee sent by the Greek National Assembly to offer the Greek throne to H.H. Prince Christian Wilhelm Ferdinand Adolf George of Denmark".

After prolonged negotiations, Greece at last had a new monarch. The young king, who was not yet 18, left Copenhagen in September and arrived in Greece at the end of October by way of St Petersburg, Berlin, Brussels, London and Paris.

At 10 in the morning on 18th/30th October 1863, the frigate *Hellas* entered Piraeus harbour. George I disembarked on the quay, where he was welcomed by the authorities of the land and the people. The royal carriage travelled by way of Piraios, Aiolou and Ermou Streets to the cathedral, where a doxology was held, after which it proceeded to the palace in Syntagma Square, where the new king took up residence in the rooms Gärtner had designed for Otto some three decades earlier. The royal family of Greece would reside in the palace until 1922, when it left it forever.

Otto's young replacement had come from a country that had been obliged to abolish its absolute monarchy in 1848 and grant the people a constitution. This meant that George, who was born in Copenhagen in 1845, had been brought up in the context of a liberal monarchy. When he accepted the throne of Greece, he was still a cadet at the Naval Academy.

The prince would undoubtedly have needed a period to adjust to his new role as a monarch, and his first years in the palace were probably not accompanied by any essential changes to the building. However, after his marriage to Grand Duchess Olga, and especially after the two became parents to a family large even by the standards of the day, modifications became essential, at least to the south-east wing.

In most of the rooms, the superb Pompeian wall-paintings and decoration were covered by cloth wall-coverings, while much of the furniture was put into storage and replaced by new items, which, though less valuable artistically, were more practical. Some of the furniture was brought from abroad, but most of it was purchased locally in Athens (the sign "By appointment to the Royal Court" frequently featured in advertisements for commercial establishments in the last decades of the 19th century) or made by teams of craftsmen and carpenters employed in the palace itself. The rooms were appointed in a style more grand-bourgeois than palatial.

Similar changes, of course, were taking place elsewhere in the capital. In the Iliou Melathron, for instance, Sophia Schliemann covered the superb wall-paintings by the Slovenian painter Juri Subic with wallpaper after the death of her husband, Heinrich Schliemann (fortunately, the paintings were brought to light once again during the recent restoration of the building and its conversion into the Numismatic Museum). Changes were also made to the Ziller residence himself after its purchase by Dionysios Loverdos. It is of little import who started the trend; what is important is that new fashions were being adopted by royalty and commoners alike across the whole of Europe in bourgeois homes, grand-bourgeois mansions and royal palaces. Modifications may also have been made to the three large reception rooms and the throne room, where George wanted to keep the Bavarian coat-of-arms which he –properly– regarded as a national heirloom.

With or without the changes, the palace remained the centre of Athenian social life, and receptions and balls continued to be held. The most splendid reception of all may well have been that given on the occasion of Crown Prince Constantine's marriage to princess Sophia. Otto had married Amalia in Oldenburg and George had wed Olga in St Petersburg, so this was the Athenians' first opportunity to see most of the royal houses of Europe assembled in their city. Accommodation in the palace was provided for the emperor of Germany

113

113. *The royal family in 1886. From left to right: princess Maria, princes Nikolaos, George, Constantine, and princess Alexandra. Prince Andreas is between Queen Olga and King George.*

–Sophia's brother Wilhelm– the empress Frederica and their retinue, as well as for the king and queen of Denmark, the Prince of Wales and his wife, Tsar Nicholas and the bride's sisters, while luxurious mansions in the vicinity were used to house the other princes. These residences were placed at the king's disposal by their wealthy owners: the mansions [megara] of Andreas Syngros (now the Hellenic Foreign Ministry), of Stephanos Skouloudis (which stood on the site of the King George Hotel), of Aristeidis Papoudov (which stood at the corner of Vasilissis Sophias and Panepistimiou Streets) and of Georgios Psychas (which is now the Egyptian Embassy). The newlyweds greeted the crowd that had gathered in the square in front of the palace from the palace's central balcony: "An indescribable wave of emotion swept through the crowd, which erupted into cheers".

The building suffered two major fires: one in 1884 which destroyed part of the north wing, and a second, more serious, blaze in 1909 –said to have been started by an oil lamp in the Orthodox chapel on the upper storey– which caused such comprehensive and catastrophic damage to the central wing and

114. *The Athens Palace. George I's study.*

115. *The Athens Palace. The reception rooms.*

116. *George I's monogram.*

its extensions into the east and west wings that repairs were out of the question. In 1931, the Venizelos administration decided to convert the palace into the seat of the Hellenic Parliament. It was thus saved, along with the 'Old Vouli', which was ultimately converted into a museum, despite calls from Professor Konstantinos Kitsikis to have the former demolished entirely and Venizelos' wish to demolish the latter and create a square. The modifications, which took place between 1930 and 1934 under the supervision of Andreas Kriezis, obliterated the final traces of Gärtner's palace.

Despite the efforts of the patrician architect and senator, Anastasis Metaxas, to have the palace restored to its original condition and used as a museum, all that now remains of this superb building is its shell, and even this has been modified, though not significantly. Virtually nothing remains of the original interior apart, as has already been mentioned, the main staircase and the trophy and adjutants' rooms. Given the present climate in favour of restoration and the work being done across Europe to uncover and conserve original wall and ceiling paintings in private mansions and palace buildings, the palace in Athens might possibly have been saved, had it only survived a little longer in its original form. Unhappily, it did not, and restoration is now impossible.

Moreover, there are very few surviving depictions (photographs, drawings, lithographs, etc.) of the palace interior under Otto or George. Gärtner's drawings, which are kept in Munich, are therefore invaluable, as are the two volumes of *The Old Palace of Athens* (the first published by the Technical Chamber of Greece, the second by the Hellenic Parliament) into which Aikaterini Demenegi-Viriraki distilled a lifetime's work.

Fortunately, the palace gardens have enjoyed a happier fate. Initially accessible only to the royal family, it was decided in 1854 to open them to the public for a few hours a day, when the royal family were not using them themselves, though not many Athenians ventured in. George loved the garden and, aided by Schmidt who had stayed on in Greece after Otto's departure, took care to enrich it with new plants. Various birds also flew freely about it, and a small zoo was created which encouraged the establishment of the zoo at Palaio Faliro. While the garden

117. *Queen Olga's bed chamber.*

118. *Queen Olga's 'rose chamber'.*

119

120

was only open to the public for two hours every Wednesday and Friday afternoon at the beginning of the century, from 1917 on, following the resignation of King Constantine and the departure of the royal family from Greece, it ceased to be a royal garden in anything but name. This situation continued after the return of the royal family which, in any case, no longer lived in the palace (apart from the queen mother, Olga, who stayed on for a short time).

In 1923, the grounds were declared a national garden and opened to the public from dawn until dusk. New paths, benches and iron seats were gradually added, all in the spirit of the original concept. Where new public entrances were created, the space was laid out appropriately, though with features of a more severe neoclassicism. Today, the garden still houses the headquarters of the presidential (formerly royal) guard in its north-east corner, whose oldest buildings date from 1868, a small coffee-house near the Irodou Attikou entrance, and a children's library in Otto's former 'hunting lodge', a pavilion designed by E. Ziller as a study for George I. A small stone house made of Hymettan marble, the pavilion was built in 1850 by Amalia, who told her father that it reminded her of a Swiss house, going on in the same letter to tell him that "I had them plant firs on the north side, to make the resemblance even greater". A second small single-storey building which Ziller also build at a later date to serve King George as a study has been used in recent years as a botanical museum.

Since 2005, the royal/national garden has been designated a municipal legal entity: the Municipality of Athens – National Garden. Although it still provides a cool, green oasis for Athens and its citizens, the queen's old garden seems to be in need of the care and loving attention of a contemporary agency with vision.

119. *The head gardener, Friedrich Schmidt's house at the corner of Voukourestiou and A. Soutsou streets (now demolished).*

120. *The Royal (National) Gardens.*

121. *The Royal (National) Gardens. The pavilion built by Ernst Ziller for King George I.*

# EPTALOFOS
# THE QUEEN'S TOWER

Queen Amalia's love of nature became clear immediately after she moved to Athens. Starting with a fairly small garden in the palace on Klafthmonos square, she then undertook to fill the square itself with plants and trees before creating the wonderful gardens beside the royal palace in Syntagma square which are now the national gardens. A large oasis of dense vegetation and a wide variety of plants (some 50,000 species), the gardens cover 15.5 hectares and are still immensely popular with Athenians who stroll there all year round.

Meanwhile, as the royal gardens were approaching completion, Amalia decided to purchase a large area of land some 8 kilometres north of the capital (near what is now Liossia) to turn into a model farm and stock-raising unit, the Eptalofos Estate. This was common practice amongst the European rulers of the day, who remained closely linked to the land through their descent from the feudal lords of old, while interest in farming and stock-raising methods was also on the rise at the time, with several treatises appearing one after another on the subject. Governor Kapodistrias had attempted something of the kind at Tiryns, where he founded the Tiryns Farm School and a model farm, while a Bavarian business man and expert in artesian wells by the name of Ruff had created a similar country estate in the late 1830s in the area of (what is now) central Athens that still bears his name. The small tower on Ruff's land at which the royal family would stop and rest when out riding is known to this day as "Amalia's little tower", and may have prompted the purchase of the Eptalofos estate.

We have evidence of similar properties in other Athenian suburbs including Sepolia, Patissia, Kypseli, Galatsi and further afield in Maroussi, Kifissia, Halandri and Yeraka. The Athenians called them "village houses" and spent the summer months there. The best known include the Amvrosios Botzaris estate, which

**122.** *Eptalofos (The Queen's Tower). Layout of the royal farm. C. Kohlmann lithographic studio. Athens. 1868. National Historical Museum.*

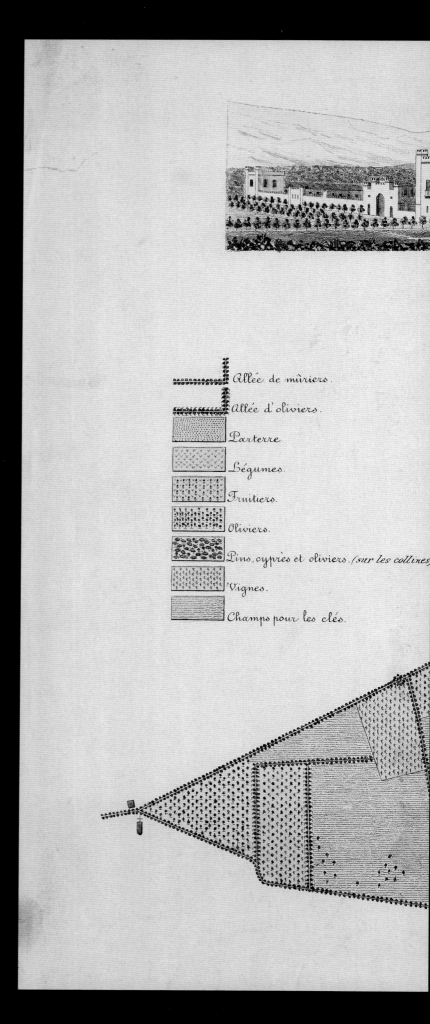

# Ferme Royale
# HEPTALOPHOS.

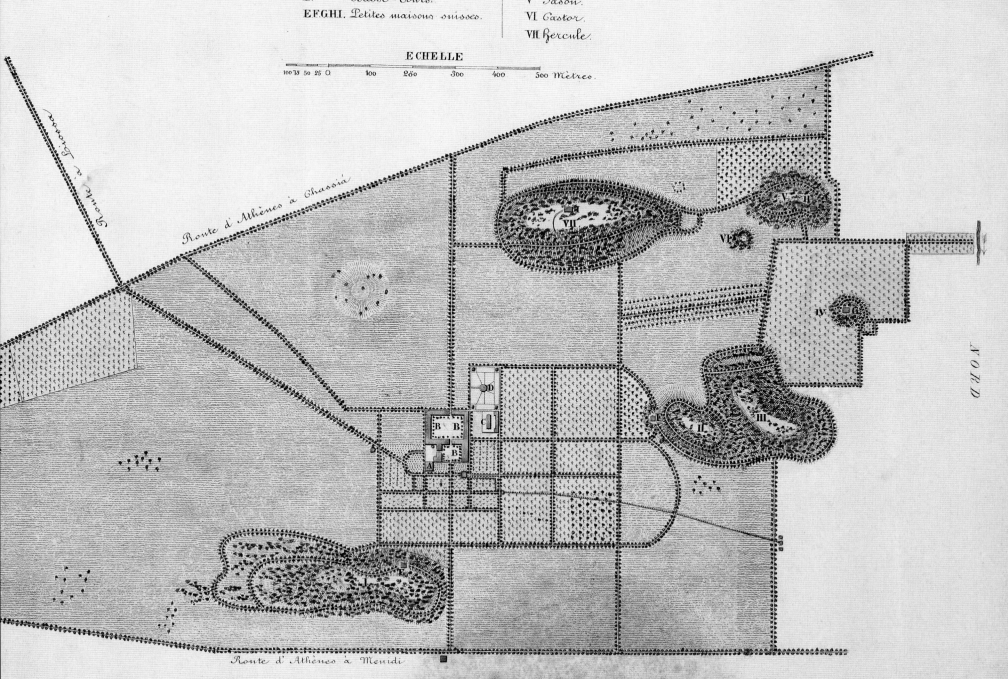

| | | |
|---|---|---|
| ⸺⸺ | Aqueduc. | Les 7 Collines |
| ⚬ ▭ | Puits et bassins. | I Orphée. |
| A. | Chateau. | II Pelens. |
| B.B.B. | Bâtiments économiques. | III Thesée. |
| C | Ecuriers. | IV Polux. |
| D. | Basse-Cours. | V Jason. |
| E.F.G.H.I. | Petites maisons suisses. | VI Castor. |
| | | VII Hercule. |

ECHELLE

100 75 50 25 0    100    200    300    400    500 Mètres.

Route d'Athènes à Chassia

Route d'Athènes à Menidi

NORD

covered 9.5 hectares beside the Petraki Monastery in Ambelokypi, and the Kifissia estate of the Epirote nobleman Oikonomidis (at the intersection of Papamichalopoulou and Mela Streets) where Otto spent the first summers of his reign (1837-1857).

Originally Turkish-owned, the estate passed into Greek and subsequently English ownership, with John Williams and George Miles planting it with vines and fruit trees, systematically cultivating the land, building new ancillary facilities and creating a fine garden. However, by the time the royal family came to purchase the Liossia estate in 1848, it was once again in Greek hands. By buying up plots of land bordering on the estate, Amalia increased its area from 30.5 hectares in 1848 to 250 in 1861. When she built a small house on it in the Gothic style, the area was dubbed the "Queen's Tower", even though Amalia herself called the royal estate "Eptalofos".

123. *Eptalofos. Detail from illustration 122.*

124. *Eptalofos. Water-colour by Angelos Giallinas.*

125. *The Hohenschwangau villa in Bavaria on which the Queen's Tower was modelled. (Das Neue Hellas Griechen und Bayern zur Zeit Ludwigo I. Katalog zur Ausstellung den Bayerischen National Museum. Munich 1999).*

126. *Room interior in the Hohenschwangau villa.*

127

128

129

**127.** *Eptalofos. The main entrance.*

**128, 129.** *Eptalofos. Photographs from the 20th century. Private collection.*

130. *Eptalofos. Photograph from the mid-20th century. Private collection.*

131. *Eptalofos. The southern courtyard with the main entrance.*

**132, 133.** *Eptalofos. The coats-of-arms of Greece and Oldenburg.*

**134.** *Eptalofos. Detail of the ceiling in the first-floor reception room.*

There is said to have been a tower in this area already, however, dating from the Ottoman occupation. Wilhelm Ernst von Beaulieu, a companion of Amalia's brother, Prince Peter of Oldenburg, tells us that the estate was known as the "Tower" in 1851, because of a building that already existed on it which was to be replaced by a new structure "in impeccable taste". This would indicate that von Beaulieu had already seen the plans for the building, or that they had at least been described to him.

This old tower is described by Edmond About as "a kind of semi-rural, semi-Gothic castle built of stone and plaster, which had a pleasantly tasteful triumphal arch in front of it". It may have been an old Venetian tower, as there were five such towers in Kifissia, which were used as country residences by the Levidis, Antonopoulos, Oikonomidis, Georgantas and Tositsas families, one in Kaisariani belonging to the Benitzelos family, another at Kareas in the foothills of Mount Hymettus, one on Mount Penteli and another on the Chasekis farm in what was then part of the Agricultural University. Since About visited Athens in 1852, when only the entrance gate had been built, his description can be taken to be fairly accurate.

The name of the architect remains unknown, though documentation has survived indicating that the Queen's Tower may actually have been designed by François Louis-Florimond Boulanger, a figure about whom little is known. An unpublished hand-written note by Boulanger in the Greek State Archives in Athens contains a memorandum addressed to Otto, dated 21 April 1853, discussing the possibility of digging artesian wells on the "royal property" to secure the water required to irrigate the estate. The memorandum is accompanied by a second, more general note on artesian wells, which Boulanger felt to be essential in an arid country like Greece. This note makes it clear that the architect began his career as an engineer working on similar projects, and that he had published some important papers on the subject in 1835 before turning exclusively to architecture and winning the Grand Prix d'Architecture. The report makes no reference to the building on the estate, and Boulanger at no point refers to it in his professional résumé.

In a short monograph entitled *The Queen's Tower*, Georgios Laios informs us that the decoration of the walls imitated that of Hohenschwangau Castle in Bavaria, where Otto was born and about which he was intensely nostalgic. In fact, Hohenschwangau is a much larger palace built for Prince Maximilian by the architect Domenico Quaglio near the ruins of an earlier, romantic palace the two brothers had discovered on an excursion to the area in 1829.

135

135. *Eptalofos. Parquet floor decoration.*

136. *Eptalofos. The Gothic-style reception room. Note the elegantly panelled walls and ceiling and the parquet floor.*

Pages 114-115
137. *Eptalofos. Detail of the ceiling in the first-floor reception room.*

Despite their considerable difference in size, the two buildings do, however, have much in common. They are both neo-Gothic buildings in the Romantic style Maximilian II had selected to transform Munich into a new and typically Bavarian capital. The Wittelsbacher Palais, the great palace built by Gärtner at the end of Maximilianstrasse in 1843, was in the same style.

The similarities between the two buildings begin with their external features (polygonal towers, battlements, arched windows, etc), continue with the gate house and extend to the interior, where there are striking similarities with both the throne room in Ludwig's palace in Munich, which was fashioned by Leo von Klenze in 1837, and with the corresponding rooms in the Wittelsbacher Palais, which were designed by Gärtner in 1844.

The building was inaugurated on 13/25 August 1854, Ludwig's birthday. It was Amalia's intention to thus thank and honour her father-in-law, of whom she was very fond and who had been forced to abdicate in 1848 as a result of his notorious affair with Lola Montez. Amalia continued to correspond with him, however, and kept him informed about progress on the estate.

The Tower's first storey was taken up by a large reception room and the bedrooms of the king, the queen and her maid of honour. A spiral staircase led up to the second storey, where there was another large room decorated with the coats-of-arms of Greece, Bavaria and Oldenburg against a vivid blue background with gold decorations. The ceiling was adorned with a lavish painting in the Gothic style featuring blue, red and gold designs. "In the tower, we have the statues from the throne room in Munich and our coat-of-arms", Amalia wrote to king Ludwig on 30 May/ 11 June 1857. Its parquet floor was laid in designs drawn up by Gärtner for the floors of the palace in Athens and by Klenze for the Wittelsbacher Palais. The walls ended in a relatively plain skirting board, while the wooden window and door frames were in the Gothic style. The upper storey was completed by two more small rooms. In contrast with the furniture in the Athens palace, which had been ordered from Paris, the furnishings of the Tower at Eptalofos were designed by F. Boulanger. This

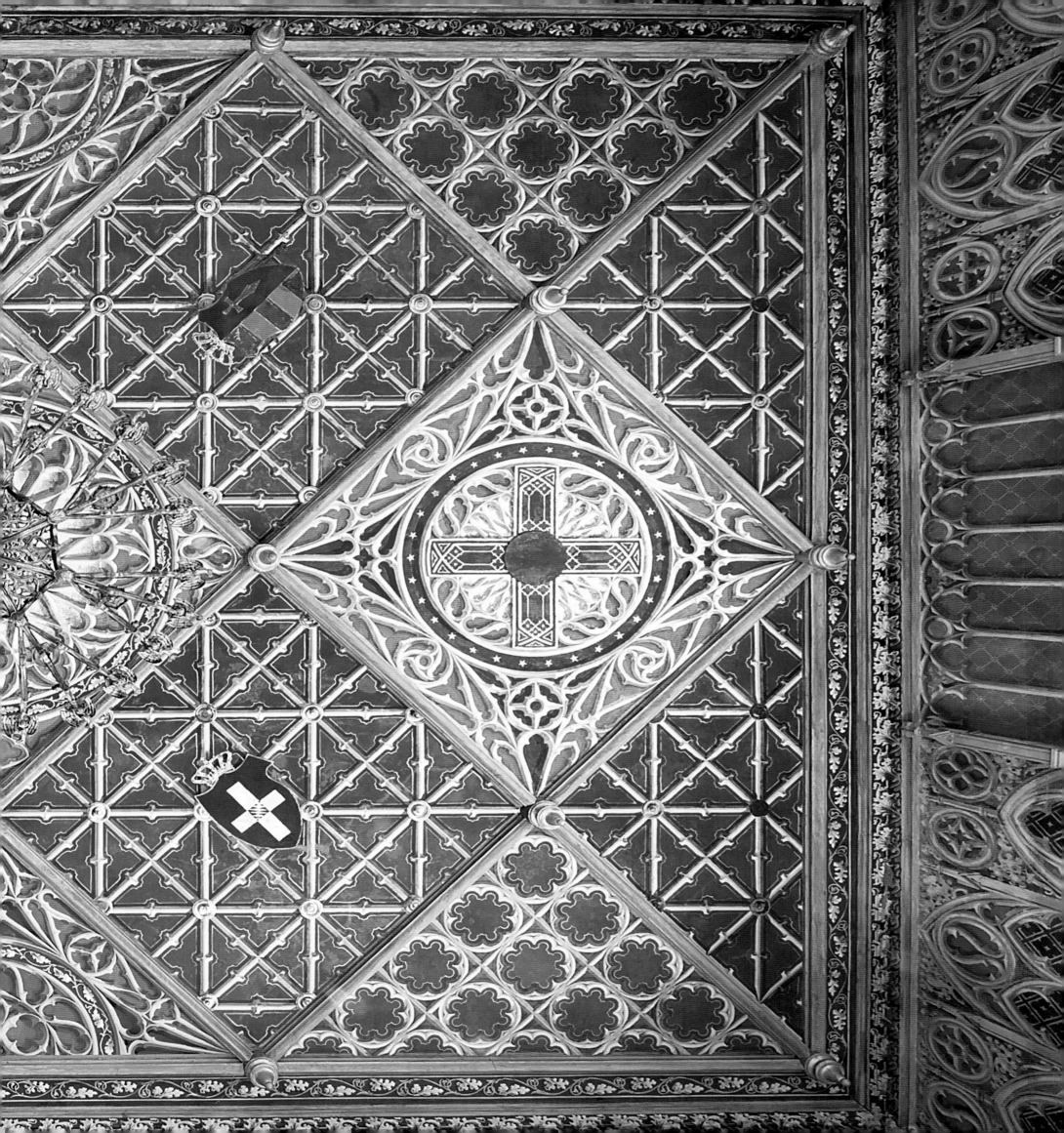

138. *Eptalofos. Gothic window.*

139. *Eptalofos. The view from the roof. The round skylight in the stairwell was probably modelled on a similar skylight in Duke Maximilian of Austria's Miramare palace in Trieste.*

information, which Marinos Papadopoulos-Vrettos included in his *The New Athens*, is confirmed by a design for furniture in the Greek State Archives bearing his signature. It would thus seem likely that the designs for the tower came from Munich, or that they were drawn up by a German architect with Boulanger simply supervising the work in accordance with the wishes and instructions of the royal couple.

Although there were other architects in Greece who could have handled the Gothic style with ease at this time –including Kleanthis, who designed the palace of the Duchess of Plaisance on Mount Penteli, Christian Hansen and Gerasimos Metaxas, who had studied in Germany– it seems to me unlikely that any of these men was responsible for the Queen's Tower.

In addition to the tower, there were a number of small, wooden pavilions on the estate built in the style of German farmhouses for the people who worked on it, while shady arbours and walks were created in the vicinity of the tower.

Eptalofos, the estate Amalia created with so much love and care, does not seem to have appealed to Otto, who, according to About, tried to buy the Duchess of Plaisance's palace on Mount Penteli in 1853, though without success. In any case, as we have already noted, Otto spent his summers on the Oikonomidis estate between 1837 and 1857, and from 1858 on at the mansion Tositsas, the benefactor of the Greek nation, had just built in Kifissia where, after church on Sundays, he would go down to the main square and engage in conversation with holidaymakers and village notables under the plane tree. N. Levidis writes in his *King Otto in Kifissia* that, on weekdays, the king would ride to Kefalari at four in the morning and swim in a cistern there. What is strange, of course, is why neither Otto nor Amalia ever tried to acquire a palace by the sea, since both were so fond of swimming. George and Olga later rented the Tositsas residence (1868) for their summer holidays.

After the expulsion of the royal family, the Greek government declared the Eptalofos estate public property and assigned its management to the Ministry of Economic Affairs, which later ceded it to the new king. The estate was returned to Otto in 1863; after his death, it was purchased first by Baron Sinas in 1870, and then by Georgios Pachys in 1878. It now belongs to Iliou SA, a farming and stock raising concern.

The Queen's Tower is of especial interest as it is the only one of Otto and Amalia's homes that has retained its interior form and decoration virtually intact; as we have seen, the conversion of their main palace into the Hellenic Parliament building eradicated all trace of both.

**140.** *Eptalofos. The fountain in the garden.*

**141.** *Eptalofos. Fount, trough and auxiliary buildings.*

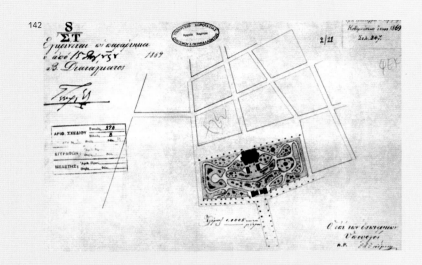

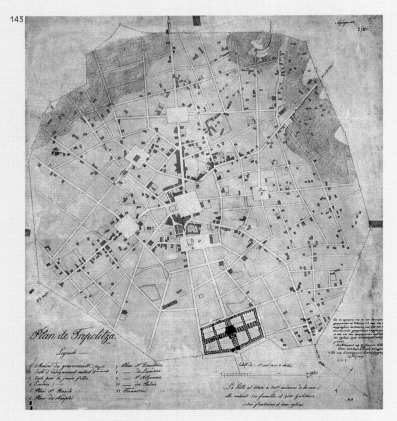

**142.** *Section of the Tripoli City Plan of 1869 depicting the site of the palace.*

**143.** *Stamatis Voulgaris and Auguste Theodore Garnot. Map of Tripoli. 1835. The site of the Government House/Palace is marked. Ministry of City Planning, Housing and the Environment - Map Archive.*

# THE PALACE AT TRIPOLI

**K**ing George visited Tripoli for the first time in 1865. The capital of the prefecture of Arkadia lies at an altitude of 633 metres and was one of Greece's finest and coolest summer resorts. Henceforth, the young king would be a frequent visitor to the area, staying with Notis Panopoulos. A year later, in November 1866, he decided to build a summer palace in the town, probably on the prompting of the civic authorities. The idea of building a palace at Tripoli was not a new one. In the town plan of Tripolitsa from 1835 (based on a design by Stamatis Voulgaris and Captain Auguste Theodore Garnot), one of the town's two main axes ends in a large formal garden with Government House at its centre. However, Kapodistrias, as was his wont, assigned priority to other public buildings, such as the school, and the design was not implemented. The municipal council ceded these public gardens to King George to be used as the site for the structure foreseen in the town's original plans. The king's adjutant, Gerasimos Metaxas, undertook to design the palace, but three years were to pass before his plans were ready.

When George married Grand Duchess Olga of Russia, the daughter of Grand Duke Constantine, the son of Tsar Nicholas I of Russia, in 1865, the rooms in the Athens palace had to be reorganised once again, particularly the day rooms used by the royal couple to which reference has already been made, and the palace at Tripoli was forgotten for a long time. The Royal Decree of August 1859 "concerning the modification of the building line of the block in the town plan of Tripoli" contains a drawing of the outline of the palace flanked by two smaller buildings, which are probably stables or coach houses. The plan of the garden diverges entirely from that specified in Voulgaris and Garnot's original town plan and follows the free layout originally associated with the English school but subsequently adopted by French designers in the 19th century: small, picturesque, winding paths and seemingly randomly placed shrubs and clumps of vegetation.

Work on the palace at Tripoli recommenced in 1869. Crown Prince Constantine had been born in 1868, and the royal family may well have continued its search for a summer residence as a result, although it is possible that the palace was a gift from the municipal authorities to the heir to the throne. However, Tripoli was too far from the capital for the king's summer residence, and the plans were abandoned once more.

George visited Tripoli again in 1898, this time accompanied by his daughter, Maria. "It was the beginning of May, the weather was fine, the trees were all in blossom and the cherry trees were heavy with the finest cherries, the excellent quality of which I admired", writes Christina Krieze Kosti, Olga's maid of honour, in her memoirs. As they drew near to Tripoli, George commented: "You'll see how fine Tripoli is. It's like a small town in Northern Italy...". The distant mountains and the fir trees reminded them both of Lombardy. George and the municipal authorities remembered the palace and decided to finish it. However, with Gerasimos Metaxas having died in the meantime, the project was assigned to his son, Anastasis.

A series of drawings (main elevation and floor plans for the first, second and third storeys), are preserved from this phase of the building. All four drawings are undated and the ground plans are unsigned, although their outlines coincide with those from 1869, which confirms that they were originally drawn up by Gerasimos Metaxas. The only drawing bearing a signature –that of A.G. Metaxas– is the elevation entitled "design for the completion of the palace at Tripoli".

It is not known whether Anastasis Metaxas made any modifications to his father's original proposal. If he did, they must have been minor changes, since the outline of the building is essential to the design as a whole. However, since the four drawings mentioned above are undoubtedly contemporary, Anastasis Metaxas must have redrawn the original design; that he only signed the elevation would suggest that his contribution was confined to this.

In effect, the building is a two-storey mansion with an elevated ground floor and an upper storey. The façades are organised in the familiar tripartite arrangement characteristic of Athenian urban mansions in the mid 19th century which reveals the influence of French *hôtels privés*. On the ground floor, the reception rooms and study are arranged symmetrically around the central hall, which ends with

144

**144**. *Tripoli. Palace Avenue. Postcard. Late 19th century.*

Pages 122-123
**145**. *A. Metaxas. Drawing of the palace's neo-Gothic façade. National Historical Museum.*

ΣΧΕΔΙΟΝ ΑΠΟΠΕΡΑΤΩΣΕΩΣ
Του
ΕΝ ΤΡΙΠΟΛΕΙ ΑΝΑΚΤΟΡΟΥ

Α.Γ. ΜΕΤΑΞΑΣ
ΑΡΧΙΤΕΚΤΩΝ ΤΩΝ ΑΝΑΚ

the main staircase. On the first floor, the arrangement is the same, the only difference being the addition of a bathroom. The bedrooms all communicate with one other via small sitting rooms and boudoirs in keeping with the French system. It is notable that although the royal family already consisted of seven members in 1898 (the royal couple plus their children George, Nicholas, Maria, Andrew and Christopher), there is only one bathroom on the first floor, which is connected to the royal bedroom, and two toilets. This makes it clear that the building was intended solely as a temporary residence. The ancillary rooms (kitchens, storerooms, etc.) were in the basement.

With its semi-hexagonal battlements in the form of turrets and ogive arches over the windows and doors, the morphology of the façade clearly references forms associated with the mediaeval period in Western Europe. Ziller, it will be remembered, was designing his country houses at this time in an –albeit less austere– neo-Gothic style, and the palace at Tripoli is very similar to the Empeirikos residence on the corner of Acharnon and Pherron streets in Athens (although both Biris and Kydonitis claim that Metaxas designed the Megaron

146

# 0
## ΕΠΙ ΤΗΣ ΚΑΤΑΘΕΣΕΩΣ
### ΤΟΥ ΘΕΜΕΛΙΟΥ ΛΙΘΟΥ
ΤΩΝ ΕΝ ΤΡΙΠΟΛΕΙ ΑΝΕΓΕΙΡΟΜΕΝΩΝ
## ΑΝΑΚΤΟΡΩΝ
ΤΟΥ
### ΒΑΣΙΛΕΩΣ ΓΕΩΡΓΙΟΥ Α΄.
Ἐκφωνηθεὶς λόγος
ΥΠΟ
### Ι. Π. ΠΥΡΛΑ
Διδάκτορος τῆς Ἰατρικῆς, Χειρ. καὶ Μαιευτ. Μέλους τῆς ἐν Παρισίοις Ἀκαδημίας, κλπ. Μέλους ἀντεπιστέλλοντος τῆς ἐν Πετρουπόλει αὐτοκρατορικῆς Ἰατρικῆς ἐταιρίας, κλπ.

Δημοσιευθεὶς δαπάνῃ
ΤΗΣ ΔΗΜΑΡΧΙΑΣ ΤΡΙΠΟΛΕΩΣ

### ΤΡΙΠΟΛΙΣ.
ΤΥΠΟΓΡΑΦΕΙΟΝ ΚΑΙ ΒΙΒΛΙΟΠΩΛΕΙΟΝ
ΙΩΑΝΝΟΥ Ε. ΑΘΑΝΑΣΙΑΔΟΥ.
1869

146. *Cover of the publication commemorating the laying of the corner stone of the royal palace in Tripoli in 1869.*

147. *Tripoli. The park in which the palace was partly built. Early 20th century. Postcard.*

148. *A. Metaxas. Drawings of the Royal Palace at Tripoli. Floor plans for a) the basement, b) the ground floor, c) the upper storey. National Historical Museum.*

147

Δ.Σ.                                                ΑΛΣΗ ΣΥΝΔΕΣΜΟΥ ΦΙΛΟΔΕΝΔΡΩΝ ΤΡΙΠΟΛΕΩΣ

Empeirikos on the corner of Panepistimiou and Voukourestiou streets, the relevant plans have now come to light in the Ziller archive: there would seem to have been some confusion over which of Empeirikos' houses was designed by Metaxas). The palace also bears some resemblance to the little palace at Chaidari which Ziller built for Nikolaos Thon, the Lord Chamberlain, in the last decade of the 19th century.

However, the palace at Tripoli was not destined to be built. The walls had risen to a height of just 5 metres when work on the palace came to a halt once again. A barrage of events following in rapid succession after the revolt in Crete and the war of 1897 produced a number of other priorities. George presented the site to the Municipality of Tripoli in 1906, and the unfinished structure was demolished to make way for Kalavryton Street when the town expanded in 1929.

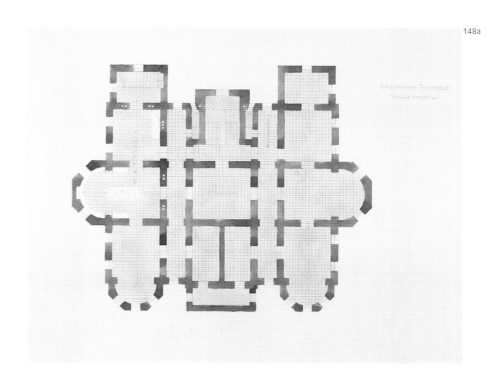

148a

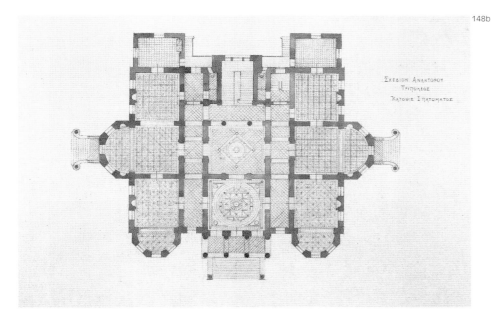

148b

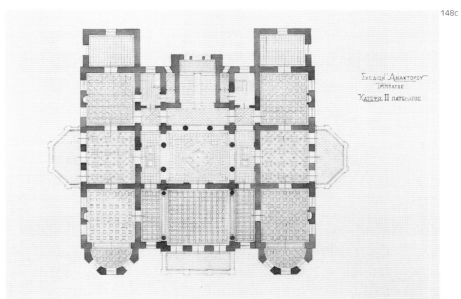

148c

149

*O BAΣIΛEΥΣ ΓEΩPΓIOΣ*

150

*H M. ΔOΥKIΣΣA OΛΓA*

**149.** *Portrait of King George I.*

**150.** *Portrait of Queen Olga.*

**151.** *Map of the Petalioi isles.*
*National Historical Museum.*

# THE RESIDENCE AT PETALIOI

he king, who was already expecting his second child, Princess Alexandra, seems to have remained preoccupied with the search for a summer residence.

George's great love was the sea, so he naturally looked for a palace close to it. Sailing was, in any case, a favourite occupation of the entire Danish royal family who holidayed every year at Fredenborg, near Copenhagen, where, together with the families of the Tsar of Russia and the Prince and Princess of Wales, they would spend their days racing boats and sailing. A summer home near the sea would have provided the opportunity for similar gatherings in Greece. It was in this context that Petalioi, Tsar Nicholas I's wedding present to Olga and George, came to the fore.

From the air, Petalioi, a small group of islands in the south-east of the Gulf of Euvoia near Karystos, looks like a colony of limpets clinging to the rocks, and this may well be the origin of the name, since *petalida* means limpet in modern Greek. The group of islands remained under Ottoman rule even after the liberation of Greece, and was the property of Omar, the Pasha of Karystos; Otto had officially recognised the Turkish régime on the islands in 1835. As we have already noted, Tsar Nicholas later purchased the Petalioi isles from Omar or his heirs and returned them to Greece as a wedding present for George and Olga. According to Ziller, the islands were handed over by means of a protocol signed by the lawyer Damianos, George's secretary and treasurer. The delegation was accompanied by the architect from Saxony with instructions to design a summer palace there, which he did.

We should perhaps mention at this point the close friendship between George I and Ernst Ziller. They first became acquainted in 1868, when Ziller came to Greece for the second time and ended up settling in Athens permanently. When the architect bought the hill covering the Panathenaic Stadium to excavate it, the King and Queen were regular visitors to the dig; indeed, the king subsequently

PETALIOU
ISLANDS.

Scale of Yards

MEGALO

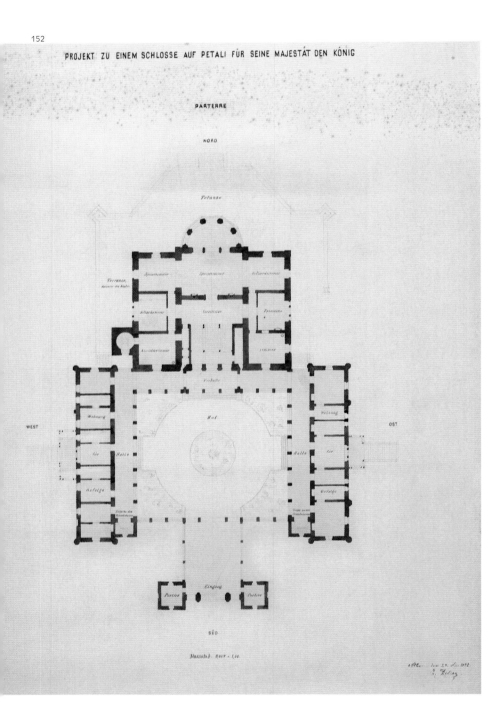

PROJEKT ZU EINEM SCHLOSSE AUF PETALI FÜR SEINE MAJESTÄT DEN KÖNIG

PARTERRE

NORD

WEST

OST

SÜD

152. *Ernst Ziller. Petalioi. Proposal for the palace. Ground level plan.*
*National Historical Museum.*

153. *Ernst Ziller. Petalioi. Proposal for the palace. View from the sea and site plan.*
*National Historical Museum.*

bought the area from Ziller and offered it to the Olympic Committee. It emerges from Ziller's memoirs that the two men frequently discussed the question of the royal summer palace. The royal couple rented two sea-side villas in the Ziller neighbourhood of Piraeus –one for the royal family, and one for the ladies of honour and the remaining staff– and spent their summers there. This is the neighbourhood so vividly described by Penelope Delta in her popular novel *Trellantonis* [Crazy Anthony], which deals with the childhood of Antonis Benakis and his siblings and has been read by generations of Greek children.

After the signing of the protocol handing over the group of islands, Ziller visited the largest –Megalo Petali (5.6 km²)– where George was contemplating building his summer palace, and proceeded to draw up two designs. A series of 5 drawings for the palace of Petalioi dated 20-25 April 1872 is now kept in the Historical and Ethnological Museum of Athens: the first is entitled "Situations Plan und Ansicht des Schlosses seiner Majest t des K nigs auf der Insel Megalo" [A topographic survey and proposal for a palace for His Majesty on the main (Megalo) island]. In the drawing, Ziller created a free garden with small winding paths and sparse vegetation on the southern point of the largest island. The general layout was cruciform, the rectangular neo-Gothic palace being in the centre with an internal courtyard and four towers at its corners. The palace was flanked by two large terraces on different levels, while in front of the building a series of belvedere terraces sloped gently down to the sea, where there was a small pavilion. A second small ancillary U-shaped building just behind and to the left of the pavilion on a naturally sheltered beach was probably meant for use as a changing room and for relaxing in. Its morphology clearly rules out the possibility of its being intended to serve as a jetty for sailing vessels, and the island's needs in this respect were probably served by an installation on the other side of the island. A road leads from the palace to the beach, while the ancillary services were located in a second U-shaped structure behind the palace. A small road leads to the mill, where there is yet another small building, clearly of an ancillary nature. The main entrance to the palace was probably on its northern aspect, where a large straight road led to a line of trees that ended

SITUATIONSPLAN UND ANSICHT DES SCHLOSSES SEINER MAJESTÄT DES KÖNIGS
AUF DER INSEL MEGALO

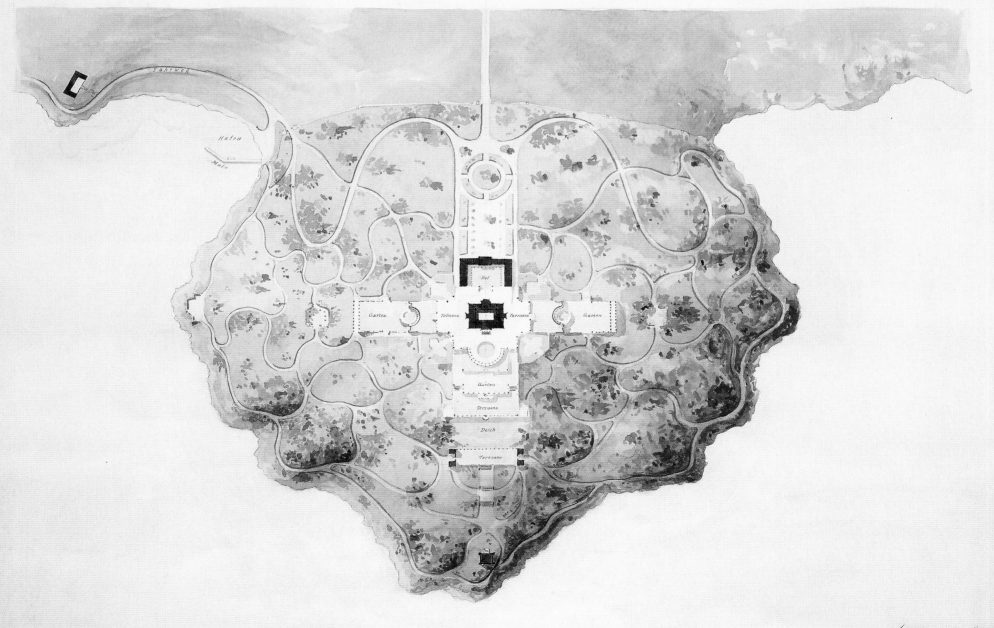

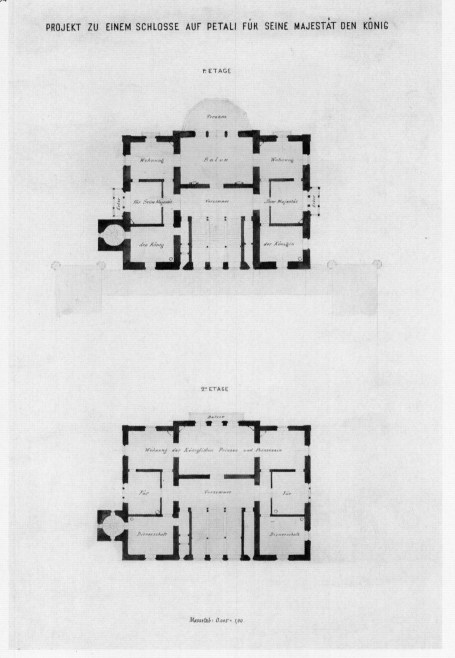

154

PROJEKT ZU EINEM SCHLOSSE AUF PETALI FÜR SEINE MAJESTÄT DEN KÖNIG

1. ETAGE

2. ETAGE

Massstab: 0.005 = 1.00

at the U-shaped building. It is not clear where boats would have anchored, or how the harbour was linked with the palace complex.

The next two drawings were produced by Ziller three days later (23 April 1872) and bear the title "Preliminary drawings for a palace on Petali for H.M. the King". The palace is oriented north-south with the entrance to the south and a view of the north. The original plan has undergone a number of changes: the dimensions of the palace have been significantly reduced and the internal courtyard done away with; the reception rooms are now on the ground floor along with a dining room with a room for storing the silverware, the kitchen office, the billiard room and the guest quarters. A large veranda near the dining room which communicated directly with the kitchen was used as an *al fresco* dining area. The new design has retained a Ziller favourite which features in several of his villas: a covered veranda in front of the sitting room leading down to belvedere terraces on a lower level. The first floor houses the apartments for the young princes, their governesses etc, while a rectangular colonnaded courtyard behind the palace houses the entourage and staff quarters.

The design of the façade is preserved in the Ziller archive in the Greek National Art Gallery. It, too, is in a neo-Gothic style with battlements, turrets and a tower on the east side of the palace. According to Dimitris Papastamos, the palace on Petalioi is virtually an exact copy of George I's family palace in Schleswig-Holstein, which was originally built as a monastery – Schleswig-Holstein, a small state sandwiched between Germany and Denmark, has both a Baltic and a North Sea coast, and still hosts the largest sailing regatta in the world. Papastamos does not clarify which of Ziller's two designs is a copy of George's ancestral palace (he probably means the second, since it doubtful whether he knew of the existence of the first), nor the name of the city in Schleswig-Holstein in which it stood.

George I's attachment to the buildings in which he lived is well-documented and is certainly no obstacle to this view. The palace at Tatoi, as we shall see, provides another example.

Ziller designed a number of similar mansions, and his Villa no. 14 is a variation on the palace he first designed for Petalioi. It was his practice to show potential clients a portfolio of villas, urban mansions, houses etc. he had already designed from which they could choose.

It is not known who requested that the first design be modified, though it may have been George himself, who would do the same later with regard to Tatoi. For his country residence, the king evidently wanted something fairly small and simple which would engender a family atmosphere, rather than something that would recall the formal environment of a palace.

There are two more drawings relating to Petalioi, both dated 25 June 1872, depicting two cottages, one intended for the estate caretaker, the other –which had a fairly large courtyard with a pigsty, hencoop, stables and storerooms– for the farmer/warden. The morphology of the caretaker's house, in particular, is reminiscent of later designs by Ziller, such as the undated Villa no. 8 which he built in Kifissia for A. Kontozoudakis, while the small farmhouse is a precursor of the sort of residence he would design for the Ziller neighbourhood in Kallithea in 1910. Ancillary buildings with a similar morphology were also built on the Tatoi estate. Although we do not know who designed these auxiliary structures, they should probably all be attributed to Ziller. We shall return to this subject later in relation to the Tatoi estate.

Petalioi, however, was not only desolate and waterless, it was also a considerable distance from Athens; when Ziller voiced his concerns about the islands and proposed Tatoi as a more suitable site for a summer palace, George agreed with him.

In the end, all that was built on Petalioi was a small pavilion which the princes used as a lodge on their hunting expeditions in pursuit of partridges and, more rarely, wild goats. It has to date proved impossible to establish whether this pavilion can be identified with Ziller's small farmhouse. Petalioi was later sold to a family of ship-owners.

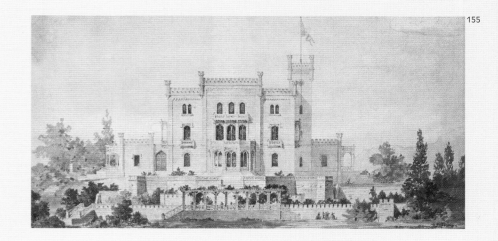

155

154. *Ernst Ziller. Petalioi. Second proposal for the palace. 23 April 1872. Plans. National Historical Museum.*

155. *Ernst Ziller. Petalioi. Proposal for the palace. Façade. Greek National Gallery.*

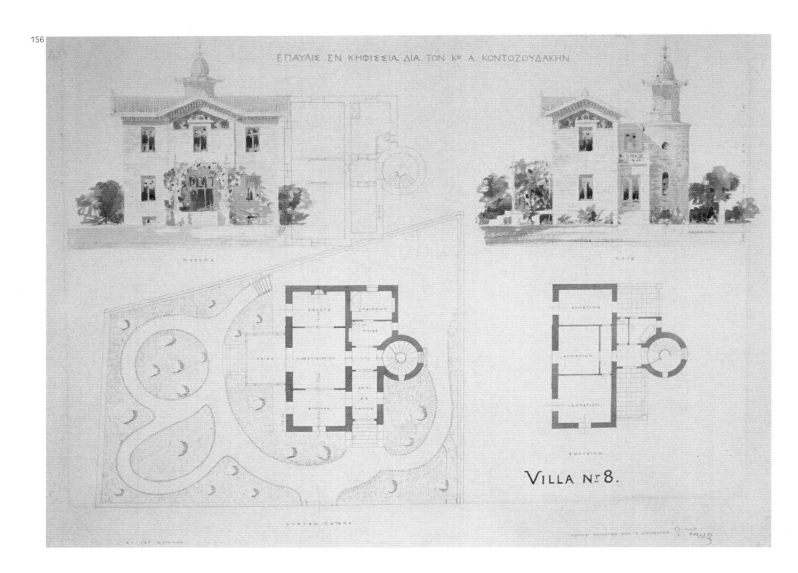

ΕΠΑΥΛΙΣ ΕΝ ΚΗΦΙΣΣΙΑ, ΔΙΑ ΤΟΝ Κ<sup>ον</sup> Α. ΚΟΝΤΟΖΟΥΔΑΚΗΝ

VILLA N<sup>r</sup> 8.

**156.** *Ernst Ziller. Drawings for the Kontozoudakis Villa in Kifissia (Villa no. 8). Greek National Gallery.*

**157, 158.** *Ernst Ziller. Petalioi. Proposal for the palace. Auxiliary buildings. National Historical Museum.*

Vordere Ansicht.　　　　Wohnung des Verwalters.　　　　Seiten Ansicht.

# Topographische Karte des Königl. Gutes Tatoi.

Die Nachtragungen nach den Angaben von K. Oldünter.

Böschungs-Maassstab.

Maassstab v. 3000 Meter.

1:12500 d. nat. G.

Signaturen.

Aufgenommen und gezeichnet im Winter 1878/79 von Obst. von Oldwig Kaupeanzs im Königl. Preus. Generalstabe.

# THE PALACE AT TATOI

s we have seen, Ziller prevailed on King George to buy the estate at Tatoi in 1871. Situated on a hill to the north of the capital, it was densely forested and enjoyed a superb view over the valley and the sea as well as summer temperatures some 5-8 degrees cooler than Athens.

"The king", writes Ziller in his memoirs, "instructed me to speak to Soutzos, the owner of the estate, and to conclude the negotiations relating to its purchase. I also offered to survey the land within a day. The estate is irregular in shape and has an area of 2,000 hectares, for which H.M. paid 300,000 Drachmas. Later, I built their majesties a temporary pavilion there in a Greek-Swiss style, which was subsequently used as a guest-house". The details pertaining to the purchase of the estate can be found in Kostas Stamatopoulos' book The *Chronicle of Tatoi*. Until then, the royal family had, like Athens' grand bourgeoisie, spent their summers in rented accommodation in Kifissia or Phreatida.

Tatoi was the favourite palace of the entire royal family, all of whom refer in their memoirs to the happy, carefree times they spent there. Princess Maria wrote: "Life at Dekeleia is much more innocent than in Athens. The royal princes run in the garden and play with their father, or take their cameras and photograph the most characteristic parts of the royal villa and groups of villagers [...]. The royal family is at its happiest in its villa beside the villagers of Tatoi. Unconcerned with court festivals and the like, and free of pedantic court etiquette, they can enjoy the scents of the countryside and breathe in the aroma of family life. [...] Tatoi is a sunny, unforgettable memory which warms my heart even during periods of the gravest grief". For her part, Queen Olga often said that Tatoi was the only place where she never felt nostalgic for 'home', while King George loved it as only someone who has created something can love.

The dates of the drawings for Tatoi, which begin in 1870, show that Ziller had dreamed of building the palace complex even before George bought the estate. This may have been the reason he persuaded the king to purchase it, given that Petalioi was so entirely unsuited to a design of that kind.

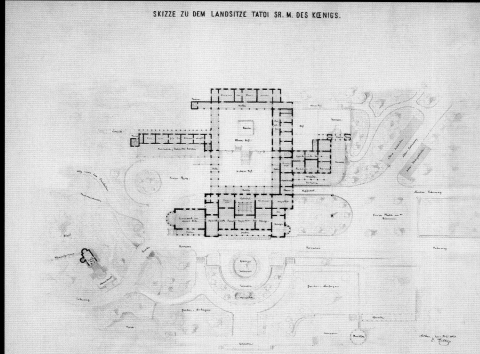

SKIZZE ZU DEM LANDSITZE TATOI SR. M. DES KŒNIGS.

160

159. *L. Münter. Tatoi site plan, 1878-1879, printed in Berlin.*

160. *Ernst Ziller. First proposal for the palace at Tatoi. Ground plan 1871. National Historical Museum.*

**Pages 136-137**

161. *Ernst Ziller. First proposal for the palace at Tatoi. Elevation, 1871. National Historical Museum.*

Ansicht

SKIZZE ZU DEM LANDSIT

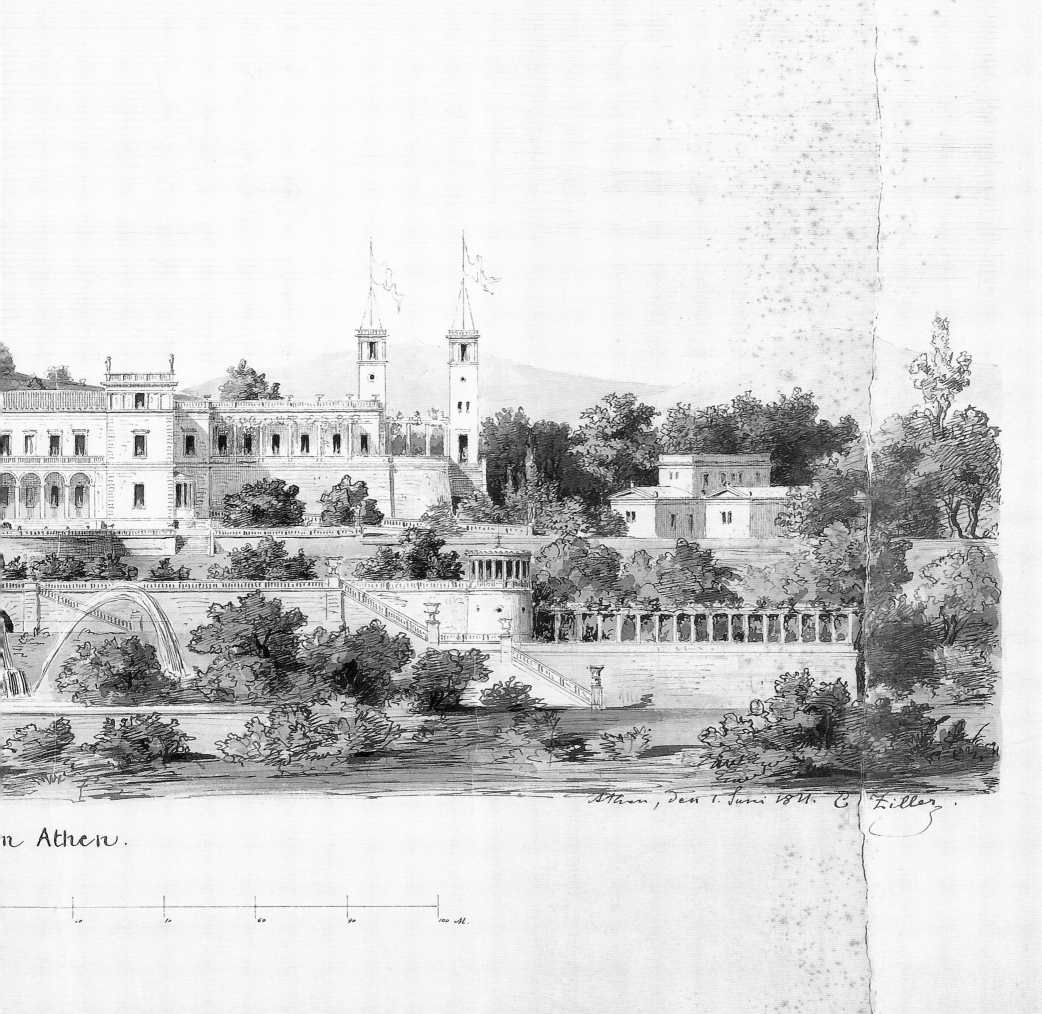

n Athen.

Athen, den 1. Juni 1841. E. Ziller.

.0        10        50        90        100 M.

TATOI SR. M. DES KŒNIGS.

162

LLA N° 14.

Despite Ziller's expectations, however, the king did not want an enormous complex; he was dreaming of something far smaller and down-to-earth: a small summer villa where he and his family could relax with their friends, far from the formalities of court. And this is precisely what he got. It is curious that Ziller says nothing more about Tatoi in his memoirs, mentioning neither the grandiose plans he had hatched for the royal palace in the summer of 1871, nor the more modest buildings that were constructed there.

Two of Ziller's drawings for his grand conception are preserved in the Ethnological Museum. One is entitled "*Skizze zu dem Landsitze Tatoi Sr. M. des Koenigs*" and depicts an extremely large palace complex with gardens on several levels, fountains, waterfalls, porticos, belvedere terraces and so on. Unfortunately, we have no precise information as to what was included in this complex, since none of the ground plans or any description of it have yet come to light; indeed, the former may never have been drawn, seeing as the word 'sketch' in the title suggests that these two drawings were nothing more than a provisional idea for a palace design. And though both are executed with great care, they are still –like Klenze's designs for the Kerameikos– nothing more than preliminary drawings. The proposal was rejected by George. There can be no doubt, however, that it was a large neo-Baroque composition rivalling Schinkel's, Klenze's and Lange's unrealised designs for the Athens palace in its flights of fancy.

Ziller envisaged a palace complex designed around a large rectangular courtyard on two levels and bounded by a colonnade. The main palace building was to have occupied one of the wings, with the entrance in the main courtyard. The king and queen's apartments and the dining room were to have been on the ground floor, with a grand staircase leading up to the first floor where the reception rooms were probably to have been located. That the reception rooms were allocated the space usually reserved for bedrooms is rather curious, and may have been inspired by George's wish to be in touch with nature and the countryside. Of course, it may equally well have been because the terraces, fountains, gardens, open spaces, pavilions and so on arranged on different levels in front of the palace essentially played the role of reception rooms.

**162**. *Ernst Ziller. Plan and elevation for Villa no. 14, a tower-like structure. Greek National Gallery.*

**163**. *Ernst Ziller: the Andreas Syngros Villa reveals the influence of Northern European castle-villas.*

Pages 140-141
**164**. *Ernst Ziller. Second proposal for the palace at Tatoi. Perspective 1872. Greek National Gallery.*

A second, independent wing set at right angles to the west side of the colonnaded courtyard was to have housed the children's apartments. Two turrets formed a small gateway at the end of this building, and there were two more towers in the complex: one at the end of the north wing, where the guest rooms were to have been located, and the other at the end of the wing given over to the servants' quarters. The latter was at right angles to the open portico on the east side of the courtyard; the guest-house is independent, opening onto its own courtyard with a small swimming pool in the middle.

Between the servants' wing and the dining room, another terrace outside the peristyle may have been intended for use as an open-air dining room, since it was located close to the kitchen. A small chapel was included to the south-east of the complex.

Here, Ziller departs from the strict limits imposed by the principles of classicism that are evident in some of his smaller buildings. As in his design for Lycabettus Hill, he gives free rein to his imagination and improvises: this is the vision of an architect who knows how to dream! After all, how often is an architect given the opportunity to build something like this?

The design probably seemed over-elaborate to George, so Ziller planned a far smaller and plainer palace: a symmetrical two-storey mansion with an elevated central section and two towers bearing the national flags of Greece and Denmark taking pride of place. As it is in virtually all of Ziller's work, the pluralist architectural concept is clear here.

The design of the building is relatively simple: the ground floor was given over to the dining, billiard and reception rooms (now on the façade) and the quarters of the king (which included a study, private apartment and bedroom) and of his valet. The first floor housed the queen's apartments (sitting room, boudoir, study, bedroom, chambermaid's quarters), while the second floor included the bedrooms of the princes and their governess as well as a number of children's dayrooms. There was also a small kitchen for basic needs. An internal courtyard enclosed by a portico linked the palace with its ancillary facilities to the north.

163

ANSICHT

PROJEKT ZU DEM SCHLOSSE TA

Tatoi d. 12 Juli 1872.  E. Ziller

...N SÜD=OST.

FÜR SEINE MAJESTÄT DEN KÖNIG.

Parterre

a. Speisesaal
b. Billardzimmer
c. Empfangssalon u. Nebenzimmer.
d. Buffet u. ...
Apartements Seiner Majestät des Königs
f. Arbeitszimmer
g. Toilettenzimmer
h. Schlafzimmer
i. Garderobe
l. m. k. ... Diener und Lakaien

## I. Etage.

Apartements Ihrer Majestät der Königin.

1. Vorzimmer
2. Empfangssaal
3. Schreibzimmer
4. Toilettenzimmer
5. Treppe nach den Apartements Seiner Majestät des Königs.
6. Schlafzimmer
7. Badezimmer
8. Garderobe
9. Zimmer für die Kammerfrauen.

## II. Etage.

Apartements der k. Prinzen u. der Prinzessin

1 Salon und 1 Schlafzimmer
4 Bonnenzimmer
1 Küche
1 Speisezimmer für die Bonnen.
2 disponible Zimmer

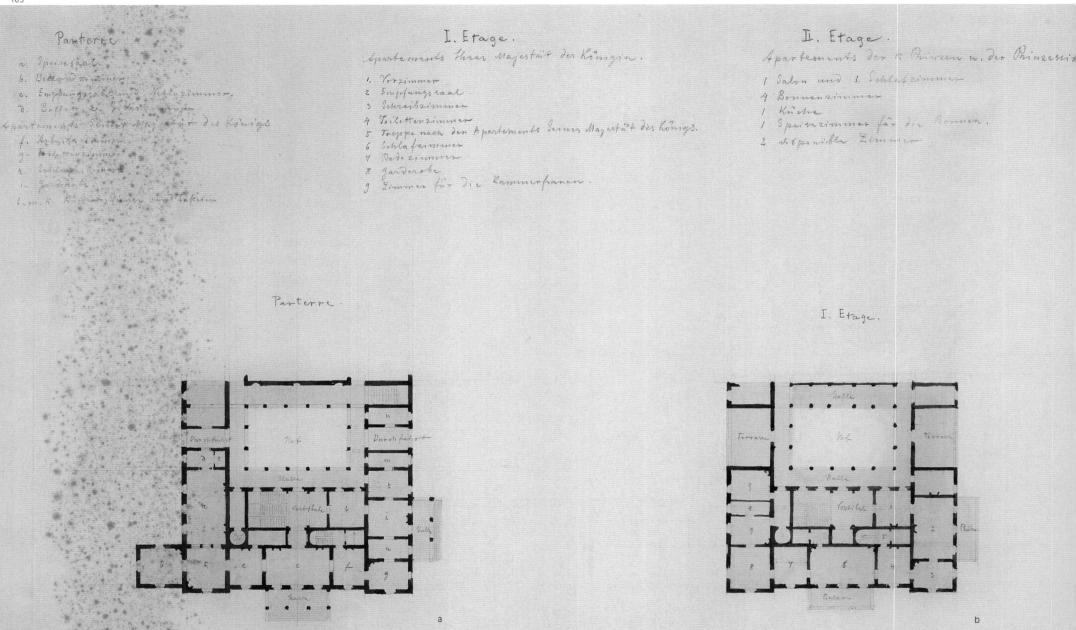

Parterre.

I. Etage.

a

b

However, this building was also judged excessive and never built (although the villa designed by Ziller for Andreas Syngros at Anavryta represents an implemented version of a very similar design).

According to Ioulia Karolou, the first Tatoi residence consisted of simple, single-storey structures that were used later as homes for the gardeners and an old villager before being demolished, a second house being built in their place. "At first", Princess Maria informs us in her memoirs, "my parents stayed in the old house, which was fairly primitive and a true village house. It's a miracle how they all managed to live in the same house with four children. But my father was an austere man who didn't allow us any luxuries and was fond of saying that we had to get used to being satisfied with the simple things in life".

It was roughly at this time that architects stopped designing large palace complexes for Greece. The idea of building palaces, the dream of every 19th-century architect and a prominent theme in virtually all the architectural handbooks and instruction of the era, began to fade in parallel with radical changes in the political and economic conditions of the western world. The focus of 20th-century architecture would shift to other subjects. The same thing occurred with church-building, though on a smaller scale.

Ziller made a number of visits to Tatoi in the summer of 1874, where he made measured drawings and sketches of the area. On 1/13 June he wrote to his siblings: "Dear brothers and sisters [...] I was recently at Tatoi and dined, as usual, with the king and queen. We ate in the open air. After the meal, His Majesty climbed a tall plane tree, sat on a branch, took (a flask?) of water from his pocket and sprinkled a little on the group. The queen shouted 'Mind you don't fall!'. Have you ever seen the king of Saxony climbing onto a fountain? But don't tell anyone about this, and don't put it in your newspaper. Please do as I say on this point.

Afterwards I played a game of cones with their Majesties. The first lady of honour joined in, along with two more ladies of honour and the king's adjutant. Later, we indulged in a spot of gymnastics, in which I excelled. I performed every exercise with the necessary courage: scissor jumps, leaps and somersaults. One

165. Ernst Ziller. Second proposal for the palace at Tatoi: floor plans for a) the ground floor, b) the upper storey. National Historical Museum.

166-168. Tatoi. The royal estate at the turn of the last century. Postcards.

169

ΤΑΤΟΙΟΝ – Η ΕΠΑΥΛΙΣ ΤΟΥ ΔΙΑΔΟΧΟΥ
TATOI – LA VILLA DU PRINCE HERITIER

"Εκδοσις της Ελληνικής ταχυδρομικής υπηρεσίας"
"Edition du service des Postes Helléniques"

**169.** *Ernst Ziller. The first villa he built at Tatoi with the additional storey added when it was converted into a residence for the Crown Prince. Postcard.*

**170.** *Ernst Ziller. Proposal for an "annex" in the Greek-Swiss style on the Tatoi estate. Greek National Gallery.*

**171.** *Tatoi: the staff building (1913-1917) to the west.*

170

lady of honour truly wanted to know how to turn a somersault, which pleased her more than anything". Whether or not the lady of honour actually learned to do a somersault, we do not know. What is certain is that the royal family lived in the small, country house with little in the way of conveniences, and that this did not prevent them from enjoying their first holidays at Tatoi.

Meanwhile, Ziller designed another small but elegant residence that was ready the following year, and in which the royal family spent their summers until 1889. Unfortunately, there are no drawings or decent photographs of this first phase of this building. The only extant photograph –which was located by Konstantinos Stamatopoulos, who has studied the estate– depicts the north-east aspect of a villa in the Greek-Swiss style which clearly had much in common with a Ziller design which is now in the Greek National Gallery, listed "Annex of the palace at Tatoi". The building also shares many features with the I. Pesmazoglou villa at Kifissia.

The house was burned to the ground during the great fire of June 1915 which reduced a large part of the estate to ashes. However, the years between its construction and destruction witnessed numerous modifications to the building, which was lengthened and had an additional storey added to cater for the needs of the ever-growing royal family. These modifications were to detract considerably from its original form.

During the period in question, similar villas and grand-bourgeois residences were often built in roughly the same style in Ziller's home town of Radebeul, many of them by his brothers' architectural practice. The central section of the pension the Ziller brothers built for their sister Helen, for instance, is strongly reminiscent of the residence at Tatoi. Buildings of this kind were said to be "in the Swiss style" in Germany; Ziller coined the term 'Greek-Swiss style' himself to reference the unique blend of neoclassical and picturesque elements in his Kifissia villas. However, he first applied the term to Tatoi at a much later date, when writing his memoirs in his old age.

A series of buildings were erected on the Tatoi estate during this same period and immediately afterwards, some of which have also been attributed to Ziller.

172

173

174

"Untere Gänslände". Partenkirchen

172. Tatoi: the little guest house known as the "royal children's school" or the L ders
residence, after the tutor to George I's sons. National Historical Museum.

173, 174. Villas in Radebeul built by the Ziller brothers. Postcards.

Built in a style commonly used for country houses in Western Europe and Switzerland, in particular, they featured the elaborate rustic ornamentation on the timber eaves, balconies and elsewhere which returned to prominence in the final decades of the 19th and the early 20th century with the rise of the Arts and Crafts movement. In Greece, the corresponding back-to-roots movement was still some time away, being a primarily inter-war phenomenon.

Tatoi's ancillary buildings –which include the Sturm house, the princes' school, the house of their teacher, Otto Lüders, the estate manager's house and the guest accommodation– has had a somewhat mixed fate, with some of the surviving structures in good and others in poorer condition.

The series of designs for the royal estate at Tatoi includes an advertisement for prefabricated villas entitled "*Chalets-Suisses*", which depicts a two-storey building of the type mentioned above. According to Stamatopoulos, George may well have briefly contemplated such a villa at Tatoi. The one advertised is made entirely of wood, however, while all the buildings at Tatoi are stone. Other, simpler buildings were gradually added to the estate to provide quarters for the staff.

By the early 1880s, the royal family had grown considerably. Crown Prince Constantine had been followed by another six surviving children (a seventh, Olga, died in infancy), and the royal villa was no longer large enough to house the family. It was therefore decided to build a new palace which –in accordance with the wishes of the royal couple– would be a copy of an English-type country house owned by Tsar Alexander II. This building, known as the 'farmhouse', stood on the huge Peterhof palace estate on the Gulf of Finland. Queen Olga is said to have spent some happy times with King George in this house, which is why she chose it as a model for the royal residence at Tatoi, though there is no documentary evidence to back this up. The building was the work of the English architect by the name of Adam Menelaus. In 1880, the royal couple sent Savvas Boukis, then a young architect, to Russia with instructions to make measured drawings of the Peterhof villa to facilitate its reproduction at Tatoi. Presumably Ziller, now an established architect, would not have been amenable to a commission of this kind.

175. *Model of a Swiss chalet made out of prefabricated timber parts. National Historical Museum.*

176. *Tatoi. Proposal for an auxiliary structure clearly in the Swiss chalet style. National Historical Museum.*

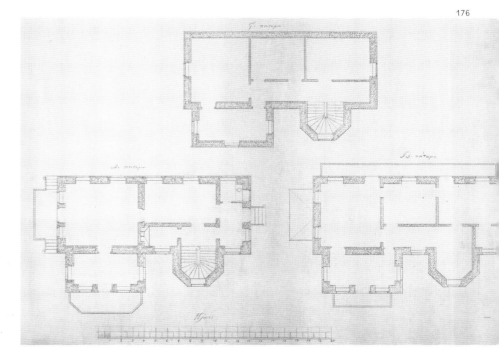

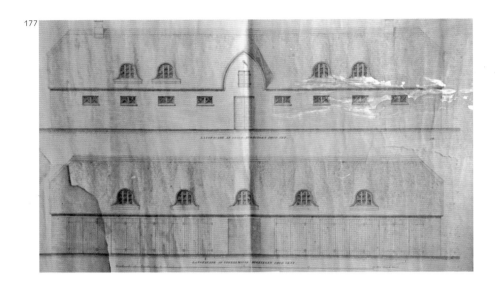

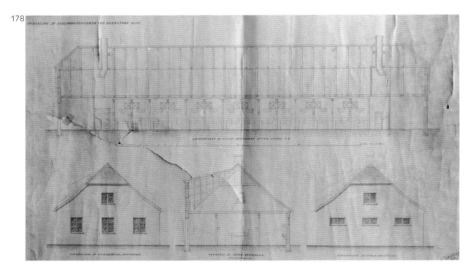

177, 178. *Models for stable buildings from the Bernsford palace. National Historical Museum.*

179. *The Peterhof farm estate: the model for Tatoi. Water-colour from 1845.*

180. *Tatoi under construction.*

181, 182. *Tatoi on a postcard from the early 20th century.*

The new palace covered an area of 1,100 m² and, together with the basement, had a total floor-space of 3,100 m². A large veranda running the full length of the façade at the ground-floor level was used by the royal family at dinner time, while Princess Maria informs us that "breakfast was served in the garden on a balcony with wrought-iron supports which was covered with ivy, roses and vines and overlooked the lake. The view from this balcony is truly superb: you can see the whole of Athens all the way down to the sea".

A double staircase led from this balcony down to a second level, where the slightly sloping garden began which contained a tennis court and a lake which was later replaced by a swimming pool. This superb belvedere terrace was not a feature of the Peterhof farmhouse, and was the only one of Ziller's proposals adopted for the new palace, though it was certainly a significant contribution.

In 1892, George invited the French landscape gardener Maton to redesign that part of the garden containing the tennis court. Today, nature has virtually obliterated the paths and turned it into a jungle, while tall trees have taken root on the court.

The Peterhof 'farmhouse' was characterised by a romantic, picturesque lack of symmetry of the sort found in English farmhouses. Its façade contained a number of disparate elements drawn from the neoclassical and neo-Gothic styles as well as traditional English country-house architecture. In making his copy, Boukis sought to imitate the model faithfully, although the fact that the original structure is plastered and the palace at Tatoi features unconcealed masonry does make a significant difference to the final aesthetic result, as does the tiled roof he preferred to the large grey rectangular slabs used on the Peterhof. The differences also extend to the form of the doors and windows, which at Tatoi employ rectangular frames in addition to the Gothic ogive lintels used exclusively on the farmhouse. The frames of the dormer windows feature intersecting circular arches which Stamatopoulos has linked to the traditional *kokoshniki* headdress worn by Russian women, though I find the comparison a little far-fetched given that similar openings are common in the English countryside – of course, Menelaus may have chosen them for that very reason,

179

180

181

182

183

183. *Crown Prince Constantine's children.*

184. *King Constantine's family at Tatoi. Postcards.*

185, 186. *Tatoi palace. United Photoreporters / N. E. Tolis Archive.*

ΑΘΗΝΑΙ - Οἱ Πρίγκηπες τοῦ Διαδόχου
ATHÈNES. - Les Princes du Prince Héritier.

184

though we will probably never know. Another of Boukis' modifications was the addition of a carved wooden band above the thin cast-iron colonnettes supporting the first-floor balconies and the roof, which served to link the palace with the other buildings on the estate.

Boukis seems to have departed even further from the original model on the villa's rear elevation to serve functional ends, while the main façade was actually at the back of the building. The end product, therefore, though resembling Peterhof, is by no means identical to it. Through a series of small but not insignificant changes, Boukis succeeded in integrating the new palace into its natural environment and in setting his own stamp on it.

The building is 72 m. long. The central wing housed the reception rooms, while the ground floor of the east wing was taken up by the king's study, library and bedroom. At the other end of the building, the front of the west wing was given over to the queen's study and bed chamber along with the bedroom of her maid of honour, while the rear housed the rooms of princes George and Nicholas. The bedrooms of the other children and their tutors were on the first floor of the east wing, while the first floor of the west wing was given over to guest rooms.

The interior of the palace was finished and decorated in the heavy, over-loaded bourgeois style of the time, and made little effort to recall a country residence – perhaps because Tatoi was used for long periods of time and not only during the summer months.

The royal family settled into the new palace in 1889, with Crown Prince Constantine moving into the residence they vacated with his family.

It was George's wish to create a model farm at Tatoi along with a dairy unit, and in this he was successful. As we have seen, in Western Europe the nobility were keen on similar projects, while both Queen Amalia, Andreas Syngros and Nikolaos Thon attempted the same in Greece at Eptalofos, Larisa and Chaidari respectively (indeed, Thon sent his son to study Agronomy in Europe so he could organise the farm).

It should be noted that great importance is attached to maintaining, conserving and restoring these ancillary farm buildings with a view to reviving the small dairy production unit at Tatoi that remained operational until well into the mid 20th century. Apart from serving as an attraction for the people of Athens, such a revival would keep alive the memory of estate life and provide a model organic food production unit.

Among the drawings from the George I Museum collections now held at the Ethnological Museum is a series depicting farm installations (stables, barns etc.) which were intended for the palace at Bernsford (designed in 1869). These drawings were probably brought to Greece as a sample. There is also a second series including stables, workshop and houses for the gardener, blacksmith, etc. which, somewhat later and much simpler, are associated with the later extension of the estate in the direction of Bafi.

By the end of the century, a small neighbourhood had been created around the royal villa consisting of a group of buildings of various sizes which are depicted accurately in a drawing from 1896 by Ioannis Pappas-Patsis.

Visitors who turn off the public road into the palace drive through greenery for a short distance before coming to the gardener's house, on the right. They then come to a small group of buildings on their left which includes the adjutant's office, telegraph office, guest quarters (second royal residence), refectory, storerooms, stables, barracks, cisterns and the wine-maker's house (the Sturm house). The construction drawings for some of these have survived. The most interesting is the adjutants' office / billiard room, which was designed by Boukis: a small, stone structure, once again a copy –according to Prince Nicholas– of a building at Bernsford. With its low wooden roof and north-European country style, it is a fine example of picturesque, rural chalet architecture. The large billiard room where the adjutants spent their winter evenings, frequently in the company of members of the royal family, is on the ground floor and has its own entrance; the first floor houses a second sitting room along with a number of bedrooms. The other drawings are mainly of smaller ancillary buildings. The royal villa, the palace and the kitchen are in front of this small neighbourhood to the right of the road.

185

186

**187**. *Tatoi palace. The inner gate.*

**188**. *Tatoi palace. The rear view.*

Other, similar buildings were added to the estate from time to time, and existing ones modified to meet new needs, making it hard to determine their use, or even their location, with any accuracy, particularly given that the 1916 fire destroyed three quarters of the estate, including Crown Prince Constantine's residence, the church of Profitis Ilias, the stables, a garage, Lüders' house, and a number of other structures. Several of these were rebuilt, most of them for new uses, though a few, such as the telegraph office, retained their original function. Today, there are twenty-nine structures apart from the palace and the chapel: the kitchen, the telegraph office, the adjutants' quarters, the house of the King's personal secretary, the partly destroyed two-storey service building, three old houses, three staff homes, the offices of the Tatoi palace guard, the gendarmerie, the Varybombi forestry service headquarters, three storerooms, the winery, the stable, the pigsty, the carpenter's workshop, the old stable, the old canteen and four garages. Many of these are in a state of near ruination and overgrown with vegetation.

It should be noted at this point that some of Ziller's drawings in the National Art Gallery may be simpler versions of original designs for the palaces on Petalioi and at Tatoi. Moreover, some of the drawings of the ceiling- and wall-paintings may conceivably be identified, after further detailed study, with rooms in the palaces at Petalioi and Tatoi and the Crown Prince's residence. A "design for a residence on the Dekeleia estate" (the subtitle has been erased and replaced by "at Dekeleia") in the Athens General State Archive depicts a small ancillary building intended for a member of the palace staff with two bedrooms and a dressing room on the first floor and a study, dining room, kitchen, WC, store-room and stable on the ground floor. The drawing is undated but signed by the "architect of the palace and the royal buildings", Anastasis Metaxas; we can therefore assume that a number of the later buildings were probably the work of Anastasis Metaxas, though the archive of this important architect has yet to be located. It is highly likely that other details relating to the remaining buildings will emerge after the George I archive in the General State Archives is opened and catalogued.

189. *I. Patsis. Site plan of the central section of the Tatoi estate. 1896.*
*National Historical Museum.*

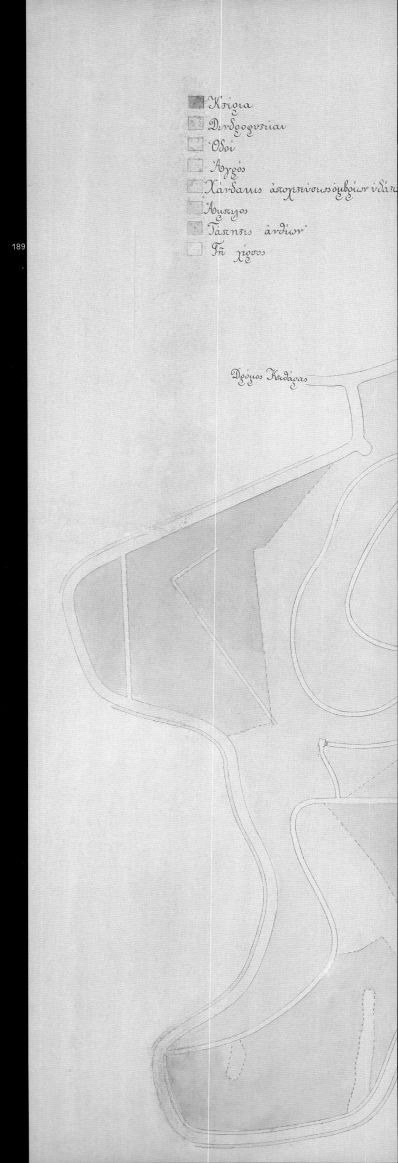

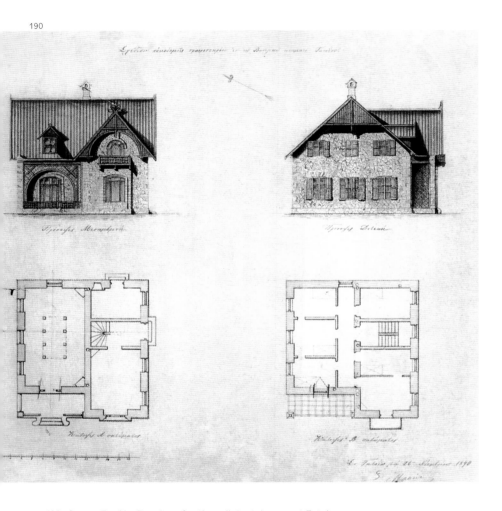

190. *Savvas Boukis. Drawings for the adjutants' room at Tatoi.*
*Benaki Museum, Neohellenic Architecture Archive.*

191, 192. *Tatoi palace. Two partial views.*

As we know, Queen Olga, the first Greek Orthodox queen, was extremely pious. During the royal family's first years at Tatoi, she worshipped in the small church of Profitis Ilias on the estate, which predated the arrival of the royal family and which the Queen had had repaired and redecorated. When the young Princess Olga died in infancy in 1880, it was decided that she should be buried at Tatoi on a small hill known locally as 'Palaiokastro'; little Olga's tomb was to mark the beginning of the royal cemetery at Tatoi.

193. *Tatoi. Flower pot in the garden with the emblem of King George.*

194. *Tatoi. Decorative marble urn.*

195. *Tatoi. A fount.*

196. *Tatoi. The belvedere.*

197. *Tatoi. The new cowshed.*

198. *Tatoi. The garage.*

**199.** *Tatoi. Winery.*

**200.** *Tatoi. Workers' housing.*

**201.** *Tatoi. Drawings for workers' housing. National Historical Museum.*

In 1899, Queen Olga conceived the idea of building a church in the Byzantine style of the church of Agios Eleftherios next to Olga's tomb; the church would be dedicated to the Resurrection of the Lord, and the royal cemetery was to be placed next to it. The church was designed by Anastasis Metaxas and the corner stone was laid on 6 August 1899 during a ceremony in which the queen, followed by each member of the royal family in turn, placed a small gold cross in the church's foundations; Prince Christopher left a silver icon. The small silver trowel that was used by each in turn to put mud onto the foundations has survived to this day. Metaxas asked the king and queen if they wished to have crypts constructed beneath the floor of the church for their eventual interment, but the royal couple refused, with George replying: "No, they will bury us out here. I want to feel the heat of the sun and the rain falling on me from the sky of my Greece". The tombs of most of the royal family are now in the cemetery at Tatoi; with the exception of Constantine and Sophia's mausoleum, the other tombs are plain and made of marble. The Benaki Museum Neohellenic Architecture Archive contains a complete series of designs for the mausoleum, which was designed by Emmanuel Lazaridis: a domed cross-in-square church measuring 6.12 x 6.12 m. externally, a small sanctuary at the east end and four columns supporting the central dome, it was originally to have had an open

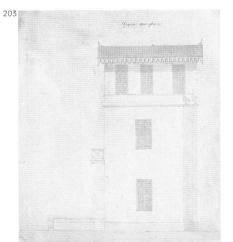

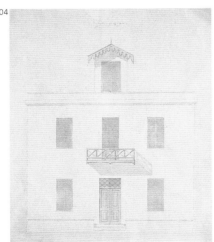

202. *Savvas Boukis. Tatoi: the guest house.*

203, 204. *Savvas Boukis. Drawings for Tatoi's guest quarters. Benaki Museum, Neohellenic Architecture Archive.*

205. *Tatoi. Officers' residence.*

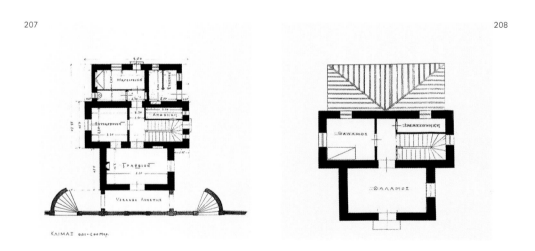

206

Ὑπόμνημα.

A. Ἱερὸς Ναὸς
B. Περιπτρόπιον
Γ. Διαμερτὰ (Στήραι)
ΔΔ. 5 ἰσόγαια κεγία ἡγεωρημένα.
ΕΕ. 11 ἰσόγαια κεγία ἄξιαι.
Ζ. 4 κεγία ἀνώγαια ἡγεωρημένα.
ΗΗ. Ἀνέσσοιοι.-
Θ. Θύρα.
ΙΙ. 2. Κυπαρίσσοι.
ΚΚΚΚ. 4. Συπεύσιοι.
ΛΛ. 2. ἀμυγδαλέαι
Μ. Καρυδία.
Ν. Καρομηχεία.

1.41 m. wide portico running around the perimeter of the building, though this was never built. The interior includes spaces for the royal sarcophagi. The series of drawings also includes the designs for Alexandros' sarcophagus, which was drawn by Lazaridis in cooperation with the sculptor Dimitriadis. The drawings are undated and were probably commissioned by George II after his return to Greece in 1935, so the remains of Constantine, Olga and Sophia –who had lain in the Russian church in Florence for the duration of the royal family's absence from Greece– could be transferred to Athens. In November 1936, the bodies were brought to Greece, where they lay in state in Athens Cathedral for five days before being buried at Tatoi on 22 November. Lazaridis must therefore have commissioned the mausoleum between George II's return in November 1935 and the arrival of the royal remains in November 1936. The bodies of Aspasia Manou and Princess Alexandra, Alexandros' daughter, have also been transferred to Tatoi from their resting place in Venice.

207                                                                 208

**206.** *Site plan of Tatoi's first church. National Historical Museum.*

**207, 208.** *A. Metaxas. Plans for a residence in Tatoi. General State Archives.*

**209.** *Tatoi. The church of the Resurrection in the cemetery.*

210. *Tatoi. The mausoleum designed by E. Lazaridis as the final resting place for Constantine, Sophia and Alexandros.*

211. *Tatoi. The tomb of George I.*

212. *Tatoi. The mausoleum.*

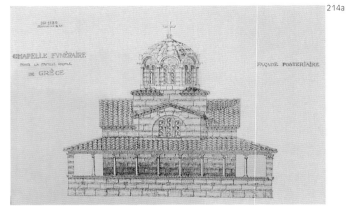

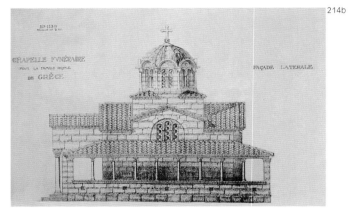

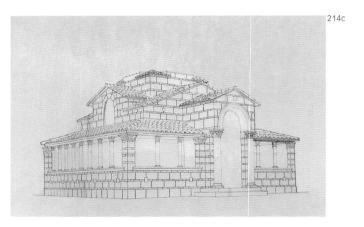

**213**. *Tatoi. Interior of the mausoleum.*

**214**. *Tatoi. Drawings for the mausoleum. Benaki Museum, Neohellenic Architecture Archive.*

**215**. *Tatoi. The mausoleum entrance from the inside.*

215

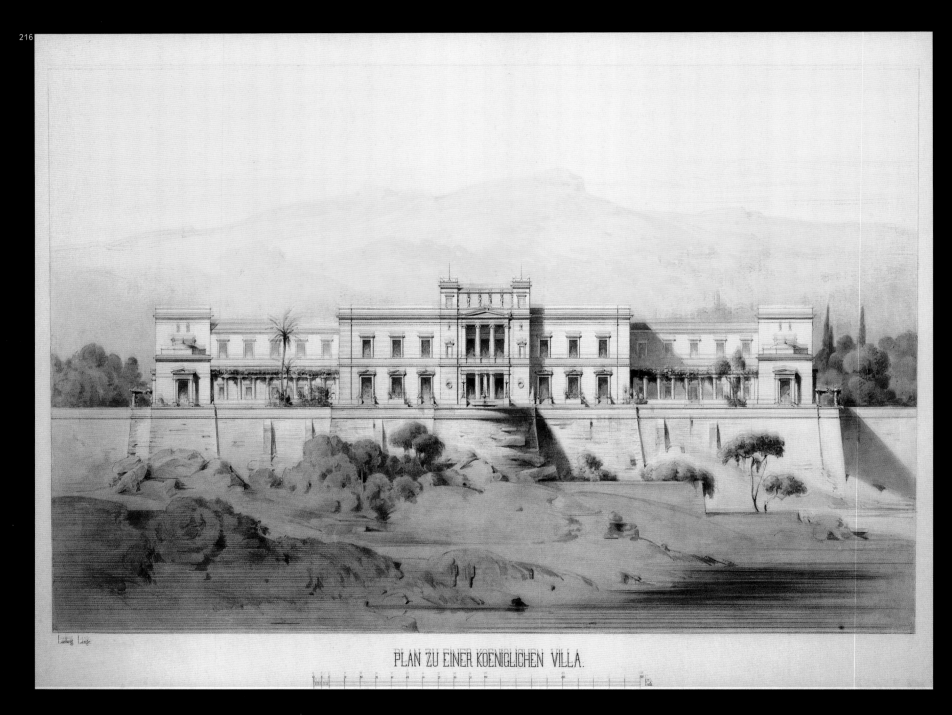

PLAN ZU EINER KOENIGLICHEN VILLA.

**216.** *L. Lange. Plan for a royal country villa. Seaward elevation.*
*Munich. State Drawing and Print Collection.*

# THE PALACE IN PIRAEUS

**T**he town plan Kleanthis and Schaubert drew up by for Piraeus in 1833 places the palace at the end of the boulevard connecting Athens and Piraeus in a commanding position on a large round plaza planted with greenery. The floor plan of the palace's central section was H-shaped and flanked by two long wings placed at an acute angle to the central section and followed the rim of the plaza and the royal gardens. A second plaza –rectangular, this time– was situated on the palace's seaward side. The two squares seem to have been connected by open arcades running through the two wings.

Klenze made far fewer changes to the Piraeus than the Athens city plan, restricting himself to suggesting a few improvements to the palace itself.

In 1835, Lange designed another mansion in Piraeus, and while he does specify its location, its distance from the sea rules out his having sited it in accordance with Kleanthis and Schaubert.

The title of the design "Drawing of a royal villa" defines both the scale and function of the building depicted: it was to be a simple country dwelling for the royal family, not a palace. A wall separated it from the sea, while Lange foresaw gardens in the French style in front and to the sides of the building: a strict geometric arrangement of round and square flower beds, paths, fountains, pergolas and two pavilions. Lange was extremely fond of pergolas and used them almost everywhere, even in his designs for the Athens Gymnasium. Lange's garden is unique among the gardens designed for royal palaces in Greece in eschewing the new ideas on the 'natural' and the 'picturesque' which had begun to supplant the rigid geometric designs popular in the late 18th century.

The royal villa was a rectangular, two-storey structure some 45 m. long and 52 wide built around an open-air atrium. Two square buildings flanking the villa on its landward side form a large courtyard with a fountain in its centre.

One side of the square was essentially an extension of the villa's landward façade to which it was joined by a long corridor; this side of the square also has

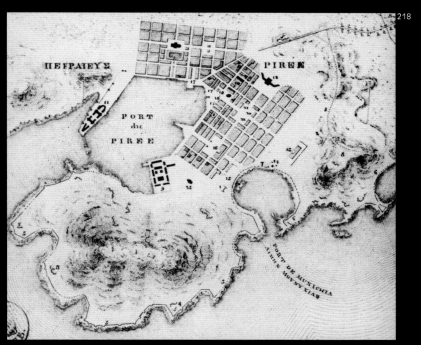

**217.** *The Ziller Quarter in Piraeus.*

**218.** *F. Altenhoven. City plan of Piraeus at Phreatida. 1837. Largely faithful copy of Kleanthis and Schaubert's plan. The palace is top right (underneath the word 'Pirée').*

PLAN
KOENIGLICHEN VILLA.

PLAN
KOENIGLICHEN VILLA.

**219.** *L. Lange. Proposal for a royal villa in Piraeus. Longitudinal section. Munich. State Drawing and Print Collection.*

**220.** *L. Lange. Proposal for a royal villa in Piraeus. Landward elevation. Munich. State Drawing and Print Collection.*

two storeys and was to house the servants' quarters. The royal stables were at right angles to this, while the other two sides consisted of one-storey buildings with large openings – closed arcades of sorts, which were designed for staff 'discussions' and games.

The ground floor of the seaward side of the villa housed more games rooms, a billiards room and sitting rooms for the use of the king and his inner circle; the remaining spaces were set aside for guests and apartments for high-ranking courtiers.

The upper storey was given over entirely to the royal apartments, with the king's salons and bed chamber on the seaward side, and the other rooms used by the king –his study, reception room, adjutants' quarters etc.– taking up one of the two wings. The other housed the apartments of the queen and her maid of honour.

The royal family's personal retinue were accommodated in the villa's two side wings above the servants' quarters. Long covered verandas (which Lange labels 'loggias') in front of the royal apartments granted an unimpeded view of the gardens and the sea.

The design is strictly symmetrical in both its floor plans and its façades, and can be described as mediocre at best. Despite Lange's efforts to create a pleasant whole with courtyards, covered verandas and arcades, the composition of these component parts reveals the architect's inexperience. It comes as no surprise that Otto rejected Lange's proposal.

As we have already seen, the royal family spent at least two summers in the late 1870s in the villas Ziller built on the shores of the gulf of Phreatida in the area known as the "Ziller neighbourhood". It is possible that these summer holidays at Kastelia set the process of building a palace in Piraeus in motion. The idea was certainly tabled around 1870.

The Greek state had made some 20 hectares over to the Municipality of Piraeus on the Peiraiki peninsula on the north-west side of Alimos (outside the limits of the town plan) on the condition that an orphanage be built there, which it was

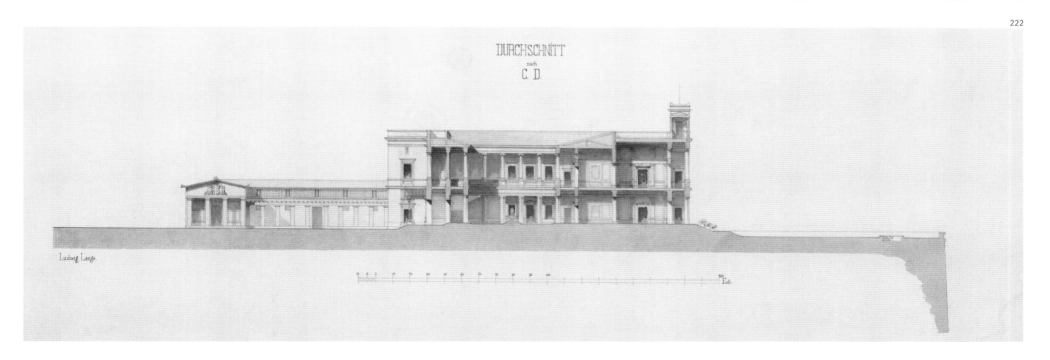

PLAN ZU EINER KOENIGLICHEN VILLA

DURCHSCHNITT
nach
A.B.

DURCHSCHNITT
nach
C.D.

Ludwig Lange

**221.** *L. Lange. Proposal for a royal villa in Piraeus. Section A-B. Munich. State Drawing and Print Collection.*

**222.** *L. Lange. Proposal for a royal villa in Piraeus. Section C-D. Munich. State Drawing and Print Collection.*

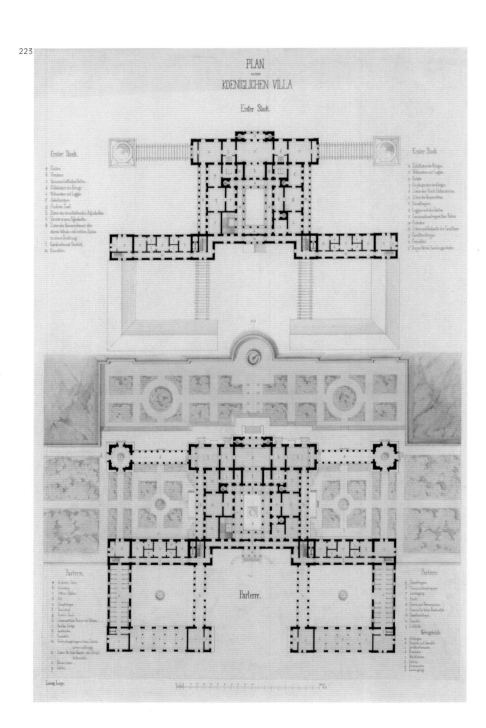

PLAN
KOENIGLICHEN VILLA

Erster Stock.

**223.** *L. Lange. Proposal for a royal villa in Piraeus. Ground floor and upper storey plans. Munich. State Drawing and Print Collection.*

(the Chatzikyriakeion orphanage). In 1876, the municipality made a gift of 25,000 *picheis* of this land to George I.

The king's land occupied a sizeable plot in what is now Peiraiki on the headland between the small harbour of Aphrodite and the bay beneath the Chatzikyriakeion Orphanage on which the Miaoulis monument stands. The area is roughly bordered by what is now Marias Chatzikyriakou Avenue and the Akti Themistokleous coast road.

The George I archive contains a design signed by H.E. Piat, the famous French architect. We know Piat worked in Athens in the mid 19th century, but little else about his activities in the Greek capital, though Andreas Syngros, who describes Piat as a fine engineer, says he had been sent to Greece by the French railroad company to take charge of their construction projects here. This may explain why, finding himself in Piraeus, he agreed to make measured drawings of the royal estate and to suggest a number of solutions.

Piat proposed two designs. In both versions the palace is U-shaped with the long sides parallel to the shore. In one version, he sites the palace near the eastern sea wall, in a second the palace stands to the west of Palaska bay, where the Naval Cadet School is now located. Two more buildings, also U-shaped, were used as stables and for other ancillary services. Piat surrounded the palace in gardens in the free English style with winding paths, pavilions and ponds for which –Piat informs us– ancient quarries were to be filled with water from wells, rainwater or the Piraeus town cistern, which stood 21 m. above sea level. He also created a number of small waterfalls. The other holes left by quarrying activity were to be filled with earth and planted with clumps of trees. Piat suggested that the stones extracted from the quarries should be used to construct the mole and the palace buildings. In both versions, the palace enjoys uninterrupted views over the sea.

"This land is of no value today", writes Piat, "and the inhabitants of Piraeus will be happy to present it to the king". And, indeed, the area, which included the tomb of Themistocles, was not occupied at that time and was not included in Kleanthis and Schaubert's town plan.

Although Piraeus had grown considerably by the mid 19th century, the land in question remained uninhabited. The city had largely expanded towards the north, where plots had been set aside for industrial development. The estate was given to George I in 1876; when the grant was confirmed by the prefecture of Attiki and Viotia in 1883, a wall was built around the property and pines and cypresses planted. Kostas Biris informs us that Stephanos Rallis offered to pay for the erection of a palace, but gives no further details.

Three proposals are now known for the palace in Piraeus. The first was drawn up by Piat a few months after scale drawings were made of the estate; entitled "A preliminary design for a royal pavilion in Piraeus", his design is dated 29 September 1876 and foresees a two-storey villa in the French style. The ground floor is again given over to reception rooms, a dining room, a smoking room, a large sitting room, etc, and also houses the royal couple's bed chamber, boudoir and bathroom; the first floor is taken up by bedrooms for the princes and their governesses, the ladies of honour and the chambermaids and bathrooms for their use. According to the notes (the plan does not exist), the basement was to contain three bedchambers and a sitting room for the staff (batman, secretaries et al.) on one side, each with its own bathroom and a shared toilet for the servants, and the kitchen, wine-cellar and queen's chambermaid's bedroom on the other, which communicated directly with the royal apartments.

The ground plan, which takes France's *hôtels privés* as its model, is cramped and even awkward, with several functional errors, the most serious is perhaps the fact that all the bedrooms on the ground floor are interlinked – while this was a common enough feature in designs for members of a single family, it certainly was not for people who are not closely related, as was the case here. Moreover, the direct link between the royal bedrooms and the main sitting room was problematic, as was the use of the two staircases at the back of the royal pavilion. All in all, the design confirms Andreas Syngros' statement that Piat was an engineer and not an architect.

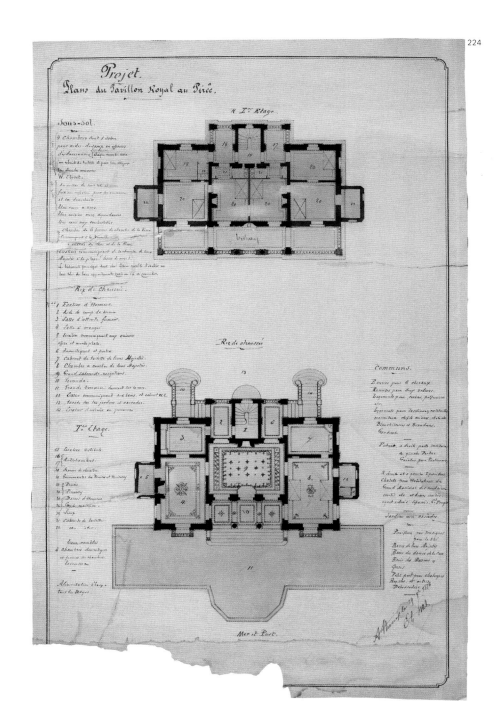

224

224. *E. Piat. Proposal for a royal pavilion in Piraeus. Ground floor and upper storey plans. National Historical Museum.*

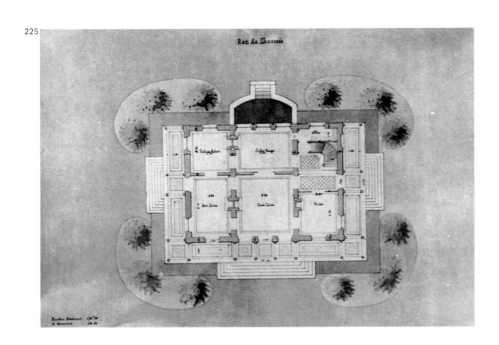

225

*Rez de Chaussée*

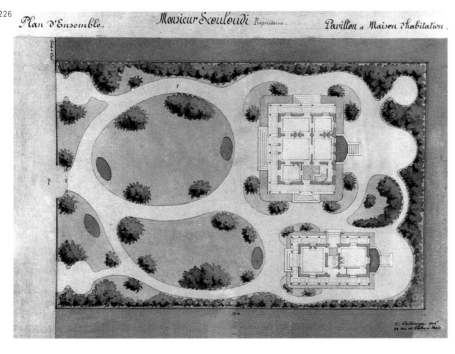

226

*Plan d'Ensemble.*     *Monsieur Scouloudi Propriétaire.*     *Pavillon a Maison d'habitation.*

On the seaward side, the main sitting room opens onto a roofed veranda, from where a broad staircase occupying the entire width of the veranda leads down to a slightly lower belvedere terrace with a fine view. The upper floor is set back some distance to create another veranda.

A second note on the right of the same drawing states that provision has also been made for stables, a carriage house with room for two carriages, staff quarters, a wash room, two *pavillons chalets* for the military commander, visitors and their consorts, gardens with waterfalls, a bandstand, a tea pavilion, separate bathrooms for the royal family, ladies and gentlemen, a landing stage for the royal launch and other vessels, and quays. The ground plan is certainly much smaller than the two proposals he originally made on the topographic survey. It would seem that, once again, George requested something smaller, which would also explain the title "*Pavillon royale*" in place of "*Palais*".

It is perhaps of interest to examine the villa designed by the French architect V.E. Poitrineau for Stephanos Skouloudis at roughly the same time in the same part of Piraeus on the site of what is now the Metaxas Cancer Hospital. Poitrineau had previously designed the Skouloudis and Vouros mansions in Syntagma square under Piat's supervision. The design here is clear: the reception rooms are on the ground floor; the veranda and the staircase leading to the rear garden begin in the dining room, of which they form an extension; the family bedrooms on the upper storey form a separate unit and communicate with each other while those on the second floor, which were used as guest-rooms, are independent. The ancillary rooms are again in the basement. The design is clearly on an altogether different level.

Another drawing, undated and unsigned, also depicts a pavilion for Piraeus. A long building in the shape of a double T, it probably formed part of a larger structure despite the absence of any obvious linking sections. The meticulous

**225, 226.** *V.E. Poitrineau. The Skouloudis Villa in Piraeus. Plan and site plan. Greek Literary and Historic Archive collection.*

**227.** *E. Piat. Site plan showing alternative locations for the Piraeus palace. National Historical Museum.*

—ΥΠΟΓΕΙΟΝ—   —ΙΣΟΓΕΙΟΝ—   —ΑΝΩΓΕΙΟΝ—

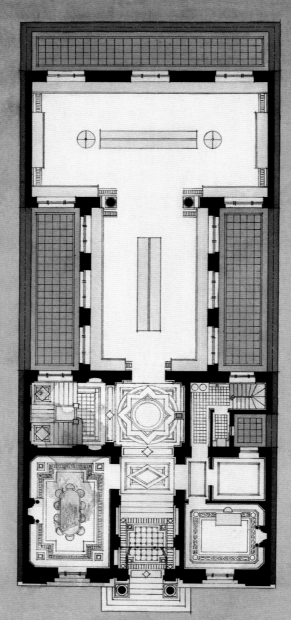
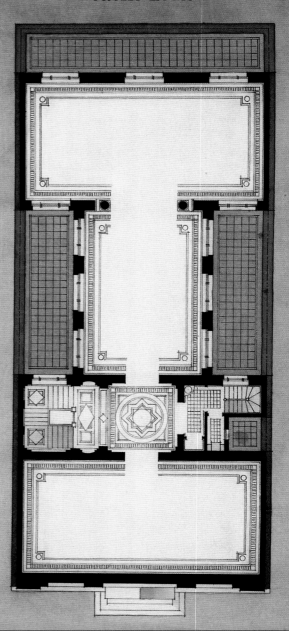

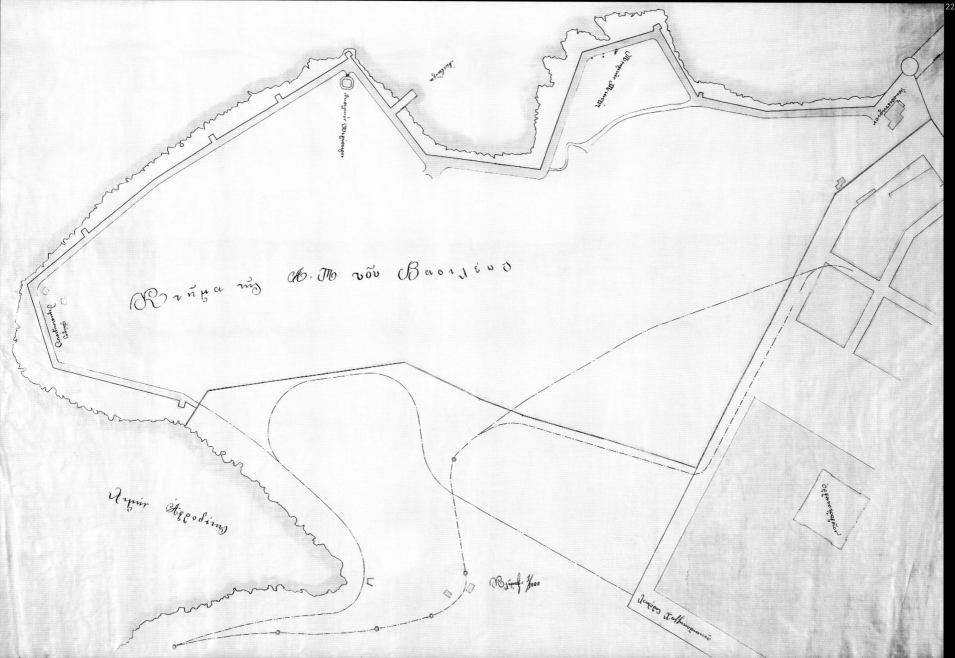

Κτῆμα τῆς Α. Μ. τοῦ Βασιλέως

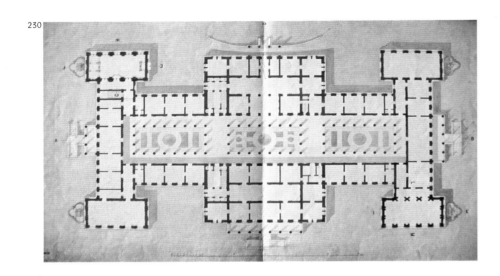

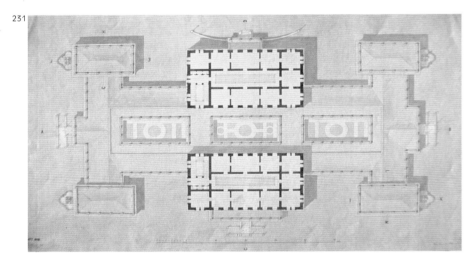

floor designs make it clear that the main residence occupied part of the basement and the ground floor of the front section of the T, while all the other rooms –that is, the upper floor of the front wing and the three levels (basement, ground and upper floors) of the main body and rear wing– contained large reception rooms. Unfortunately, the drawings are not annotated, and we have to deduce what exactly is being depicted; it may well have been a separate structure entirely.

The third and most substantial study for a palace in Piraeus is the well-known design by Hansen, which the architect presented to the then prime minister of Greece, Charilaos Trikoupis, in 1889 as a gift to king George.

At the end of the 1880s, Theophilus Hansen's study for the reconstruction of the palace in Copenhagen, which had burnt to the ground, aroused George I's interest in a summer palace. Russac states that Hansen made three visits to Greece during the 1880s (in 1887, 1888 and 1889) and designed the palace in 1888, while he was in Athens to deliver his designs for the Library in person, largely because his rivals had begun to scheme against him. It was at this time, according to Russac, that he decided to design a palace near the sea for George. In the topographic survey preserved in the Vienna Academy of Fine Arts, the palace is located in the royal section of Piraeus, on roughly the same site chosen by Piat twelve years earlier.

The site plan is rather hastily prepared. Nevertheless, a letter from Hansen to his friend the Danish architect Ferdinand Neldahl (which was found in the Copenhagen Architectural Archives by A. Papanikolaou-Christensen, who kindly gave me permission to publish it) seems to suggest that Hansen was not sure of the palace's precise location when he was designing it; all he knew was that it would be near the sea, "because the king is a born sailor". He thus seems to have designed the palace first and then located it in Piraeus, between the two small bays of Aphrodite and Palaska. This is confirmed by his letter, in which he writes: "I have not designed the stables, because, you see, I do not know where the palace will be built" and also by the claim that he had prepared ten drawings (three ground plans, two elevations, two longitudinal sections, a perspective

232

233

plan and a cross-section of the ceremonial chamber and the chapel). He does not mention a site plan, which was probably drawn up later when it was decided to site the palace in Piraeus, thus accounting for the makeshift nature of the design. The letter to Neldahl is dated 1886, exactly two years before the date mentioned by Russac, though this is clearly an error: the date is written at the bottom of the page in a different hand, and may have been added incorrectly by Neldahl at a later date.

Hansen's design for a large complex with interior peristyle courtyards is somewhat similar to the palace designed by Klentze for the Kerameikos. Hansen claims that he was inspired by the houses built by the Greek colonists in Pompeii, and concludes that the Athenians should build in this same manner in their mother city.

The building essentially consists of a large rectangular single-storey structure rising to two storeys at the corners, which project slightly, and to three storeys in the two "middle" buildings, as he calls them, which also project forward in the middle of the long sides. The four buildings at the corners have hipped roofs, while the two in the middle, one of which was used as the royal residence and the other as a guest-house, have large rectangular glass openings in their roofs to light the inner courtyard, which also rises to three storeys. A large balcony on the first floor of the royal residence, directly above the main porch, was for the use of the king.

According to Hansen's own description, the basement of the building was intended for ancillary rooms: kitchens, storerooms, cool rooms, the cook's residence, etc. The courtiers' rooms were on the ground floor of the two long wings; the reception rooms in the two short wings, again on the ground floor.

**234.** *T. Hansen. Proposal for the Piraeus palace. Cross section. Vienna. Academy of the Fine Arts.*

**235.** *T. Hansen. Proposal for the Piraeus palace. Section of the royal chapel. Vienna. Academy of the Fine Arts.*

**236.** *T. Hansen. Proposal for the Piraeus palace. Longitudinal section and cross-section of one of the four corner structures in the NW corner of the complex. Vienna, Academy of the Fine Arts.*

**237-239.** *T. Hansen. Proposal for the Piraeus palace. Samples of wall and ceiling decoration in the royal apartments. Vienna. Academy of the Fine Arts.*

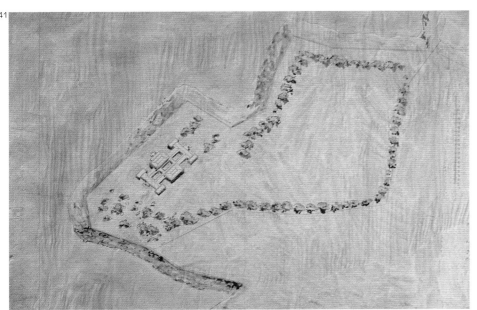

**240**. *Theophilus Hansen (1813-1891).*

**241**. *T. Hansen. Site plan of the Piraeus palace. Vienna, Academy of the Fine Arts.*

Three corners of the building were occupied by three large sitting rooms (*c*. 20 x 10 m.), while the fourth was given over to the palace chapel whose interior (Hansen informs us) was in the Byzantine style – meaning it had a central sanctuary at its east end flanked by a prothesis and a diakonikon) though it was no different externally from the other corner apartments. It should be noted that Hansen had prior experience of the conventions of Orthodox church design thanks to his involvement with the church of the Holy Trinity in Vienna.

Communication between the rooms on the ground floor was external by way of the linking passageways in the large porticos and peristyles, which faced onto the courtyard in the manner of Pompeian houses.

As we have seen, the building was sited beside the sea, from which it was separated by only a narrow jetty. However, with the exception of the large porch that opened onto the staircase leading to the jetty, the large balcony attached to the royal apartments and two smaller rooms above the porches at each end of the building, it did not face the sea. It is basically an introspective building, with a double gateway leading to the main entrance at the rear of the palace.

Trefoil flower beds arranged around a large statue were laid out on either side of the two porches which opened onto the garden at the mid points of the two ends of the building, in front of the corner reception rooms and chapel. The integration of the building into its environment does not seem to have concerned Hansen – which was only natural, seeing as he did not know where the palace would be located when he designed it. Instead, he focused on the building itself: "There will be a lot of colour in the building", he wrote to Neldahl, "a polychromy that is called Pompeian, but which I call Greek. It will be the first time a palace has been built with Pompeian wall-paintings, with all its rooms full of Pompeian colour".

But what did Hansen mean exactly? It is extremely unlikely that he was unaware that Gärtner had decorated the palace in Athens with wall-paintings influenced by the excavations and restorations at Pompeii, or that his friend and pupil E. Ziller had already decorated both Heinrich Schliemann's residence, the famous Iliou Melathron (1881) in Athens, and his own residence in Mavromichali Street

(1882) in the same manner. Perhaps he was alluding to the building as a whole, including the internal courtyard, colonnades, etc. Even the internal courtyard of the "middle" buildings recalls that of the Melas mansion [Megaron], where the teacher clearly imitates the pupil. I would venture to add at this point that, although he was not aware of it himself, Hansen's designs for the palace in Piraeus were influenced by the Venetian *palazzi* along the Grand Canal in Venice, which he had visited a few years earlier. Moreover, in 1858, Georgios Sinas, father of Simon, had bought the famous Palazzo Grassi in Venice and despatched Hansen to renovate the building (Venice remained under Austrian occupation until 1886). It is not impossible, therefore, that Hansen was influenced by his impressions from this visit. This hypothesis is supported by the Venetian feel of a watercolour depicting the Piraeus palace from the sea with its boats sailing in front of the small wharfs, reflection of the building in the water flanked by tall fine greenery, even by the dimensions of the boats, which recall gondolas, and especially by the hues used.

The palace at Piraeus, a plain building with neoclassical façades, is possibly one of Hansen's finest works. Here, as in the Zappeion Megaron and the Library, his is a flexible interpretation of neoclassicism.

The Danish architect's remarks about George I in his letter to Neldahl are very interesting. Having said that he considered it his duty to reintroduce the Greek style into the country that had given it to the world, and having stressed his pleasure that five major buildings had now been built to his designs in Athens (the Dimitriou mansion, the Observatory, the Academy, the Library and the Zappeion Megaron) and that the old tradition of art had been restored, he writes that he feels it incumbent on him to design a country palace for the king of Greece. However, since the king has displayed little interest in Greek art, he writes, he was thinking of meeting the heir to the throne —who was studying in Germany and would be returning to Greece by way of Vienna (in fact, Constantine had been sent to study in Germany in 1887 and returned to Athens in 1888 to marry Kaiser Wilhelm's sister, the princess Sophia)— and giving him a guided tour of the Austrian capital in order to show him his work and to present

242, 243. *Piraeus in the late 19th century. Postcards.*

his views. It is not known whether he actually did so, but the Crown Prince's palace (now the Presidential Mansion) which Ziller designed a few years later was clearly influenced by the forms of the façades of the "middle" building in the royal residence in Piraeus.

In the summer of 1888, Hansen wrote to Hans Auez, a professor at Berne Polytechnic: "my involvement with the Greek palace has just come to an end; this study gave me great pleasure. Now, however, I have to look to my old age. I cannot thank God enough that, despite my seventy-five years, I can still work for eight hours a day. For true pleasure in life lies in work, and in the happiness of the people around you".

However, the palace in Piraeus was also destined never to be built. All that was constructed was a small mole, a central pavilion and two small houses, "one at a mid point along the coast road with a balcony and glass windows around it", the other at the entrance to the pavilion. However, the royal family would often visit them and spend several hours enjoying the view of the sea. They usually celebrated the first day of Lent there with a number of guests. It was also to this small pavilion that the royal family came by sea aboard the royal launch *Dangar* to receive the distinguished guests arriving in Athens by way of Piraeus to attend Constantine's wedding.

One more sketch of part of the façade of the three-storey building is included in the George I archive with the Greek flag with Saint George flying from its roof. The drawing is entitled "A view of the neoclassical coastal palace". It might be a proposed design for the royal kiosk, but no positive identification has yet been possible.

In his will, George I bequeathed the estate to Prince Andrew. The land reverted to the Municipality of Piraeus in 1922, and became the property of the Piraeus Port Authority in 1931. The estate was open to the public; closed for a time due to vandalism, it is now open to the public once more.

244. *Unsigned, undated plan for a royal pavilion by the sea. The Greek flag with Saint George flies above it. National Historical Museum.*

245

## CH. HANSEN'S DESIGN FOR THE SUMMER PALACE OF H.M. THE KING OF GREECE

**T**wo designs by Christian Hansen for a summer palace are to be found in the manuscript section of the National Library of Greece. The drawings are signed, but nothing more is known about them.

According to A. Papanikolaou-Christensen, who first published them, they date from 1865-1880, when Hansen had left Greece after many years in Athens (1833-1850), initially for Trieste and subsequently, in 1857, to take up a professorship at the Academy of Fine Arts in Copenhagen, where he was also appointed Inspector of Public Works.

Although there is no firm evidence, it is likely that he stayed in touch with Greece, either through friends or through his younger brother, Theophilus, who as personal architect to Baron Sinas was commissioned to build first the Athens Academy, which was completed in 1886, then the Zappeion (on the death of F. Boulanger) in 1879-88 and the National Library, 1887-1902. He was therefore well informed about what was happening in Greece, and would have learned of King George's wish to acquire a summer palace. It would not, in any case, be surprising if this had appeared in the Danish Press, since the doings of the young king, a prince of Denmark, were of interest to readers in his native land. In the absence of any other information, however, it is not known whether the design was intended for Petalioi, Tatoi or Piraeus, or if it had been preceded by some written or verbal understanding with George, either in Denmark, which the king frequently visited, or elsewhere.

The design is for a square two-storey building measuring 50 x 50 m. with an internal courtyard at the second-floor level. The entrance is approached by a double staircase. Because of the slope of the terrain, the basement forms a solid base along the main façade, which is divided into four horizontal zones: the lower two of rusticated masonry, the upper two plastered.

The façade is divided by horizontal string courses which mark the division between the storeys. The window frames are plain at the ground floor and

245. *Christian Hansen (1803-1883). Portrait, probably by his brother Theophilus. Royal Library, Copenhagen.*

246

247

crowned with pediments on the upper storey. Hansen placed Corinthian pilasters between the windows on the corners of the upper storey, while the pilasters are Ionic in the central section, which is recessed to create a 20 m. long balcony. The interior details are interesting, and can be seen in the section drawings detailing the Pompeian wall-paintings in the upper-storey rooms. The tympana on the pediments above the windows in the courtyard arcade are painted with the same mermaids with forked tails and confronted griffins which Hansen's brother Theophilus used for the railings of the Grand Bretagne Hotel.

The austere neoclassical building is perfectly in keeping with Athenian classicism but not fully integrated into its environment—though, as we have seen, Hansen probably did not know where the summer palace was to be sited. His brother Theophilus would encounter this same problem later when designing the "Piraeus Palace".

246. *C. Hansen. Proposed summer palace for King George I. Elevation. National Library.*
247. *C. Hansen. Proposal for summer palace for King George I. Section. National Library.*

# THE PALACE OF THE CROWN PRINCE (PRESIDENTIAL RESIDENCE)

Crown Prince Constantine was betrothed to Princess Sophia of Hohenzollern, the daughter of Kaiser Frederick of Germany, in 1888; the marriage took place the following year. The young couple initially moved into the Louriotis mansion in Amalias Street, which was designed by Troump and Piat. However, the Greek state, which had promised, on his birth, to present the prince with a residence of his own when he came of age, now acted on that promise.

The design of the new palace was assigned to Ziller. It was suggested that it should be sited on the land behind the royal palace which had been used until then as the royal vegetable garden. Ziller was instructed to produce a palace that reflected the ideology of the young couple, who wanted to be close to the people and at one with the Greek environment in which they lived. This meant that the Crown Prince's palace should not differ greatly from the residences of the capital's grand bourgeoisie, particularly since the cost of it would be borne by the citizens themselves.

It is generally accepted that Princess Sophia's views carried great weight in the design of the palace, although the former king Constantine of Greece claims that George I took all the decisions alone, without asking his son's opinion. I am inclined to agree with him for two reasons: firstly, because Constantine and Sophia were both still very young (Constantine was only 20 and Sophia 18), while Sophia did not even live in Greece; and secondly, because Sophia would have incorporated the ballroom from the outset, and not when building was already underway, if she had played a pivotal role in the design and construction of the palace, which began in 1891 and was completed in 1897.

The initial drawings of the Crown Prince's palace have not been found, and may have been given to King George I or Crown Prince Constantine. What does survive in a private archive is a series of drawings included in an exhibition of

249

250

248. *The palace of the Crown Prince (Presidential Residence).*

249. *Ernst Ziller (1837-1923).*

250. *Prince Constantine and Princess Sophia. Sketched by M. Reichan. Engraving from Le Monde Illustr , 1889.*

**251.** *The palace of the Crown Prince (Presidential Residence). The front elevation and the entrance ramp.*

**252.** *The palace of the Crown Prince (Presidential Residence). The Ionic columns in the main porch (detail).*

Ziller drawings at the Stratigopoulos Hall in January 1939. While a large number of the 370 drawings recorded in the catalogue are now kept in the Greek National Gallery –A. Soutzos Museum, an equal number are now missing– presumably those sold during the course of the exhibition. The file originally contained twenty-four drawings of the Crown Prince's palace, one (a proposal) of the royal villa at Tatoi and one of the royal villa on Petalioi (the drawing mentioned above, which is now in the Ziller archive in the Greek National Gallery – A. Soutzos Museum). Seventeen of the twenty-four drawings relating to the palace in question have now been located. Those in the private collection have numbers at the top right corner, which were added at a later date and correspond with those in the exhibition catalogue, which makes it easy to identify the missing drawings, which detail the entrance staircase, the ballroom and the gardens and stables.

Another drawing by Ziller, which is now kept in the archives of the National Theatre of Greece, depicts the ground plan for the ground floor of the Crown Prince's palace with the ballroom added. This drawing is probably contemporary with, or even slightly earlier than, the previous series, from which it differs in only a few points: the form of the rear part of the ground plan, and the fact that the dimensions of the annex are noted. This drawing is of great interest, since it illustrates the ceiling paintings for the rooms, which may enable them to be identified with several unidentified watercolours dated 1892 and 1897 in the Ziller Archive at the Greek National Gallery – A. Soutzos Museum, as well as with a number of undated drawings.

The drawings are annotated in Greek, while the corresponding drawings in the series in the private collection are in German. The two sets of annotations are identical in content.

In the ground plan and –especially– the façades, the Crown Prince's palace is very similar to the central section of the Piraeus palace designed by Hansen. The main Ionic porch on Irodou Attikou Street leads into the main entrance hall where the large, striking staircase begins as a single staircase before dividing on a landing into two separate flights leading up to the first floor. The staircase is lit from

ΑΝΑΚΤΟΡΟΝ ΤΗΣ Α.Β.Υ. ΤΟΥ ΔΙΑΔΟΧΟΥ

ΕΞΩΤΕΡΙΚΗ ΝΤΖΑΜΟΘΥΡΑ        ΕΞΩΤΕΡΙΚΗ ΘΥΡΑ

**253.** *Ernst Ziller. The palace of the Crown Prince. Drawings for the entrance (outer gate and inner gate elevations and plan). Private collection.*

**254.** *The palace of the Crown Prince (Presidential Residence). A door on the first floor.*

above through a large glass light panel supported on twelve Corinthian columns. As one enters, the king's apartments are to the right: the Crown Council chamber (now the office of the President's personal assistant), the King's study (a large corner room with a view over the garden, which is now the office of the President of the Republic), the main bedroom, a small sitting room and the adjutants' room. On the left, there were two more rooms, a sitting room and a family room, along with the refectory which communicated with the basement kitchen by way of a spiral staircase. The rear wing housed the rooms of the service officers and a second semicircular staircase allowing communication between all the storeys, from the basement to the second floor. The original open-well of the staircase was replaced in the mid 20th century by an elevator.

The imposing staircase leading up to the first floor is decorated with a large mural depicting King Constantine I on horseback painted by George Scott in oils (1914). The work includes the king's brothers behind him, also on horseback; Constantine is wearing a black armband in mourning for the death of his father, George. The border of the painting lists the victories of the Greek army crowned by laurel leaves.

A large corridor leads to the reception room and ballroom in the west and north wings, while the south wing is taken up by the personal rooms of the Crown Prince and his consort, the bedrooms, the library and a number of small sitting rooms enjoying a view over the garden. There are also some smaller ancillary rooms towards the back of the building. The bedrooms and playrooms of the royal children and their tutors are on the first floor, whose ceilings were considerably lower than on the ground floor. The basement houses the kitchen, storerooms and other ancillary rooms.

When the royal couple first moved into the palace in 1897-1898, they already had three children —Georgios, Alexandros and Eleni— and the family would continue to increase in size over the years to come with the births of Pavlos, Eirine and Katerina. This may have been one of the reasons why Queen Sophia asked Ziller to add a large new ballroom on the ground floor around the turn of the century, so as to free up the rooms on the first floor for daily family use.

With the exception of four which relate to the initial building phase, the Ziller drawings in the afore-mentioned series belong to this period and relate to this construction phase. There are two versions of the proposals which differ radically with regard to the roof of the large new ballroom which the architect tacked on to the end of the palace, parallel with modern Vasileos Georgiou Street, in order to leave the garden facing Lykeiou Street free. The new room, which measured 9.15 x 34.25 m., is at ground-floor level and is connected with the main building by means of a single-storey annex with a large internal square courtyard with a glass ceiling to provide lighting and ventilation for the courtiers' dining room on the ground floor, which the extension had transformed into an internal room. It is not known whether this small internal courtyard was ever built, but it certainly does not exist today. A large part of the courtyard was taken up by a small recess in the ballroom, the upper part of which was used to seat an orchestra, and by various other smaller structures that transformed this pleasant area into a light-well.

These conversions were probably carried out much later, in the mid 20th century, when another large reception room was added as an extension to the ballroom, again along Vasileos Georgiou Street, which was known as the Credentials Room and was linked to Ziller's room on its east side. The precise spot where Ziller placed the slightly elevated orchestra stand was later used for the royal chapel.

The two different versions of the ballroom roof are particularly interesting: one is hipped, the other a vaulted metal structure measuring some 10 x 24 m. This was a very advanced structure for its period, and provides further proof that, in addition to being a very good architect, Ziller was also a very fine engineer.

The sectional drawings depict the lavish nature of the interior decorations; it is not known whether these were ultimately implemented, though if they were, they have vanished forever as a result of subsequent repairs, conversions (under George II, the interior decorator and architect Patrinos is known to have made significant changes to its interior) and modifications made to conform with current fashions.

254

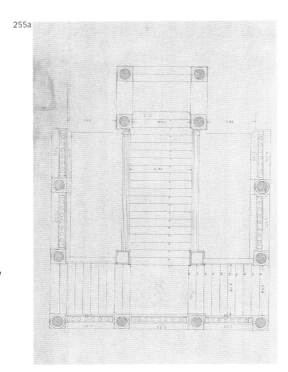

The three storeys are distinguished clearly on the façade by means of string courses encircling the building at the appropriate levels. On the second-floor level, marble metopes bearing the national emblem and the initials K and Σ (for Constantine and Sophia) are placed between the double windows that emphasise the order (all these features were also used by T. Hansen on his design for the Piraeus palace) along with mythological scenes in relief. The entire building is covered by a flat roof whose parapet has balusters and pillars adorned, at its four corners, with statues depicting winged Victories. There was only one balcony originally, above the main entrance porch, but the roof of the room linking the building with Irodou Attikou Street was used as a balcony for the first-floor dining room after the construction of the ballroom.

In both its exterior and interior, the building reveals many of the architectural details that reveal both Ziller's great attention to detail (fireplaces, floors, window casements, string courses etc.) and his talent for combining neoclassical elements with eclecticism to produce buildings which avoid being heavy or prolix and exude a delicate grace.

**255.** *Ernst Ziller. The palace of the Crown Prince. Drawings for the main staircase. Private collection.*

**256.** *The palace of the Crown Prince (Presidential Residence). The main staircase leading to the upper storey.*

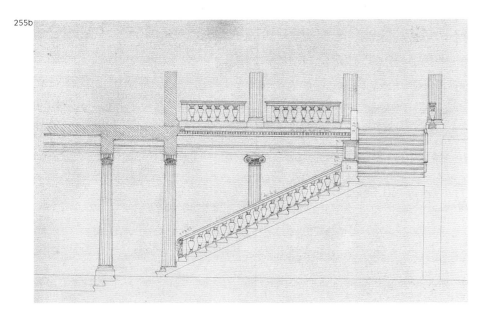

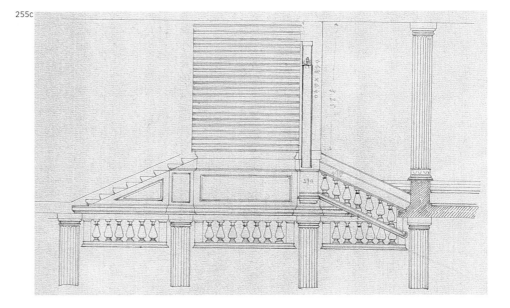

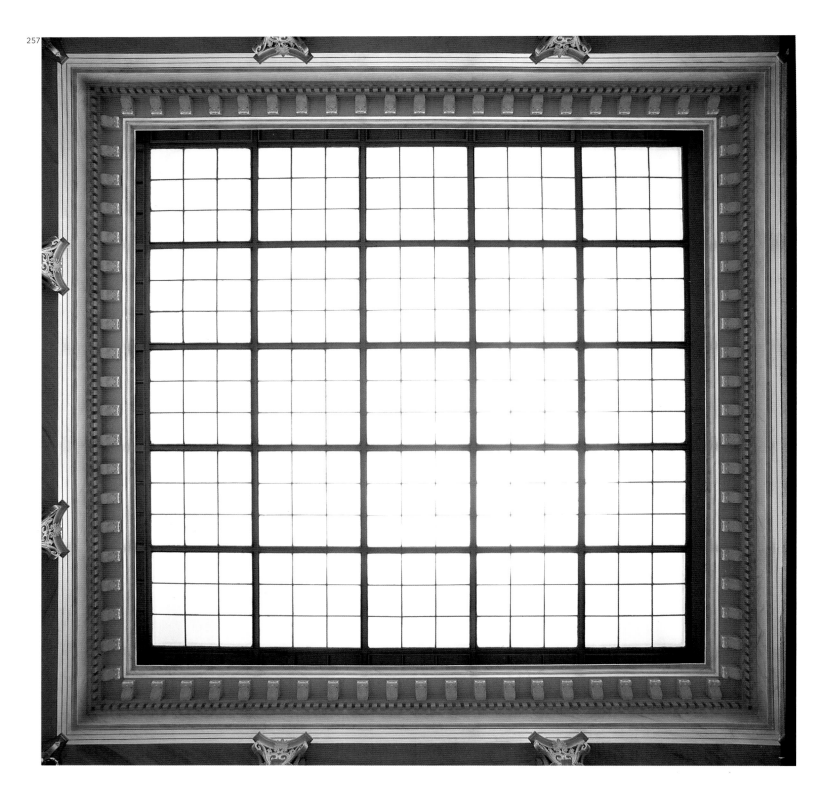

257. *The palace of the Crown Prince (Presidential Residence). The glass roof over the main staircase.*

258. *The palace of the Crown Prince (Presidential Residence). View of the main staircase.*

**259**. *The palace of the Crown Prince (Presidential Residence). View of the main staircase.*

**260**. *The palace of the Crown Prince (Presidential Residence). Main staircase. Detail.*

261, 262. *Queen Sophia with princess Aikaterini (left), and with the royal children: Georgios, Alexandros, Pavlos, Eirini and Eleni (right). Period postcards.*

Overall, the Crown Prince's palace is an austere neoclassical three-storey building, no larger than the Athenian bourgeois mansions designed by Ziller at this same time for Melas, Koupas and Vougas.

On Christmas Eve 1909, a large part of the royal palace in Syntagma Square (which now houses the Hellenic Parliament) was destroyed by fire. While repairs were carried out over the next three years and from time to time later, the entire royal family lived in the Crown Prince's palace which had to serve as Athens' 'temporary palace'.

The mansion on Irodou Attikou Street was used as a royal palace from 1913 until Constantine II's departure from Greece during the Colonels' dictatorship (1967-1974). While the king was in exile (1924-1935), it was used as a government building. Since 1974, it has served as the official residence of the President of the Hellenic Republic.

The building has not been significantly altered over the years, though, of course, the current layout does deviate in places from the original ground plans. However, while most of the modifications are to be expected, since the palace has been in continuous use for an entire century, some others, particularly those made after the restoration of democracy in 1974, which include the installation of a jacuzzi on the first floor, seem bold, possibly absurd and certainly not in keeping with the architectural values of a building of this kind.

The main ground-floor modifications are the addition of a staircase at the rear of the building to permit communication between floors without the use of the main staircase, and the addition of an elevator. A second elevator was added when Georgios Papandreou was Prime Minister. A number of toilets have also been installed.

The other rooms have remained basically as they were designed, give or take the occasional partition. Perhaps the most significant interventions have been the removal of the semicircular ramp at the entrance, the extension of the porch, the conversion of a window into a door leading directly into the garden, and the creation of a second staircase in the centre of the south side near the King's

**263**. *G. Scott. King Constantine on horseback. Oil painting on the first floor of the Crown Prince's palace.*

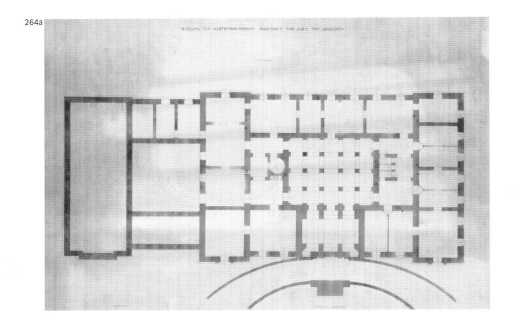

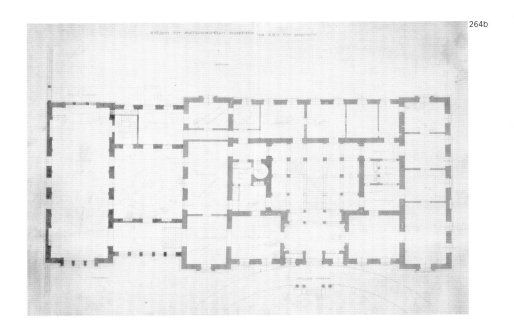

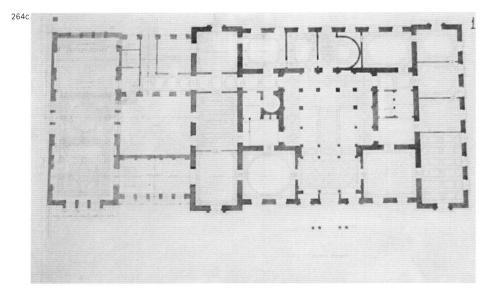

**264.** *Ernst Ziller. The palace of the Crown Prince.*
*Addition of the ballroom. Floor plans for:*
*a) the basement,*
*b) the ground floor,*
*c) the upper storey.*
*Private collection.*

**265.** *Ernst Ziller. The palace of the Crown Prince. Drawings for:*
*a) the rear elevation,*
*b) the southern elevation,*
*c) the rear elevation, version II. 1890.*
*Private collection.*

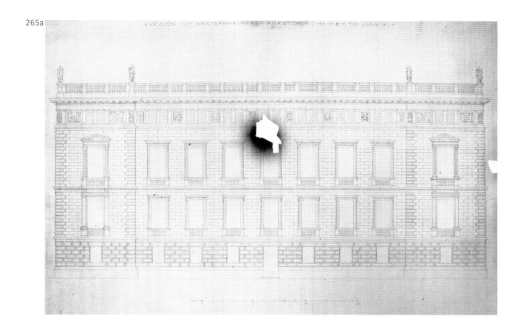

265a

265b

265c

266a

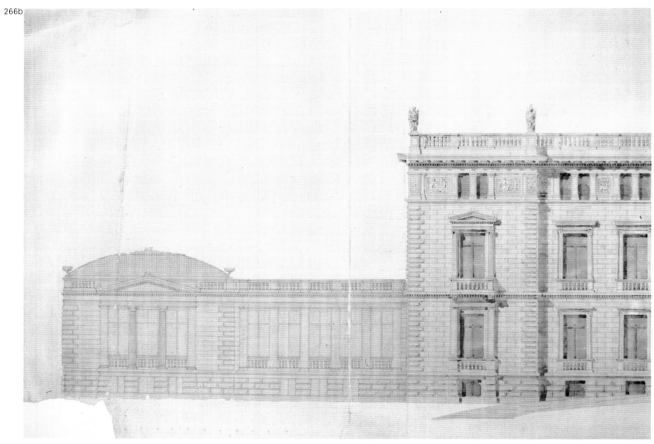

266b

**266.** *Ernst Ziller. The palace of the Crown Prince.*
*Addition of the ballroom. Front elevation.*
*a) Version I.*
*b) Version II. 1890.*
*Private collection.*

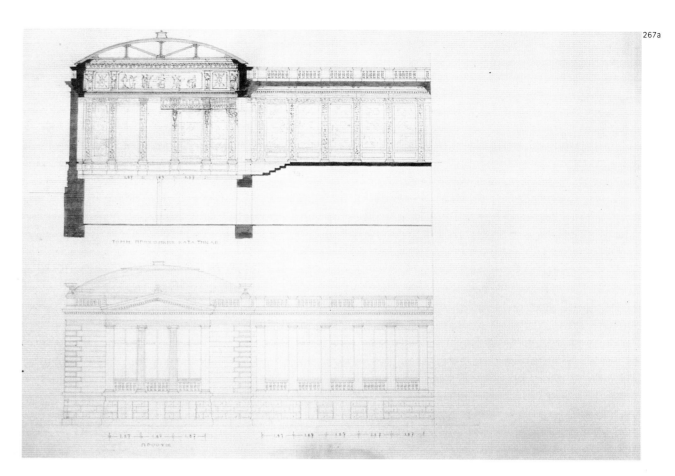

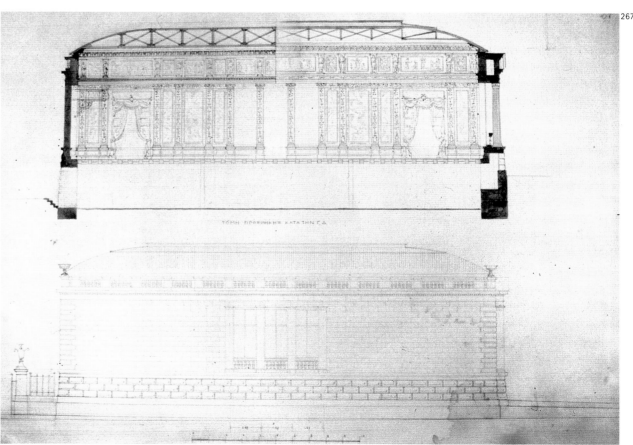

267. *Ernst Ziller. The palace of the Crown Prince.*
*Addition of the ballroom.*
*a) Cross section and façade, version II.*
*b) Longitudinal section and side view, version II. 1890.*
*Private collection.*

**268**. *The palace of the Crown Prince (Presidential Residence). The reception rooms on the first storey.*

**269**. *The palace of the Crown Prince (Presidential Residence). The King's study (now the office of the President of the Republic).*

270

(now the President's) apartments from which the President of the Republic welcomes his guests on 24 July, the anniversary of the restoration of democracy in Greece in 1974.

Similar changes have also been made on the first floor, which originally housed the king's quarters and a number of reception rooms, and on the second floor, where the royal children's apartments were.

King George was assassinated in 1913 and work on the restoration of the palace in Syntagma Square ground to a halt. On 5 May, Constantine was sworn in as king and the Crown Prince's palace was transformed into the King's residence. In 1933, the palace in Syntagma square was repaired and converted into a new home for the Hellenic Parliament.

**270.** *The palace of the Crown Prince (Presidential Residence).*
*The reception rooms on the first storey (detail).*

**271.** *The palace of the Crown Prince (Presidential Residence).*
*Antechamber to the Ball room and the new hall added in the 20th century.*

**272**. *The palace of the Crown Prince (Presidential Residence). View of the ballroom.*

**273**. *The palace of the Crown Prince (Presidential Residence). The new hall added in the 20th century.*

**274**. *The palace of the Crown Prince (Presidential Residence). Front elevation (detail).*

**275**. *The palace of the Crown Prince (Presidential Residence). Carved mythological scenes in relief on the second-storey metopes.*

**276**. *The palace of the Crown Prince (Presidential Residence). Detail of the second-storey metopes.*

**277, 278**. *The palace of the Crown Prince (Presidential Residence). Constantine and Sophia's monograms on the second-storey marble metopes.*

279. *The palace of the Crown Prince (Presidential Residence). The staircase leading to the garden added to the king's quarters.*

280. *The palace of the Crown Prince (Presidential Residence). The garden alongside Irodou Attikou Street.*

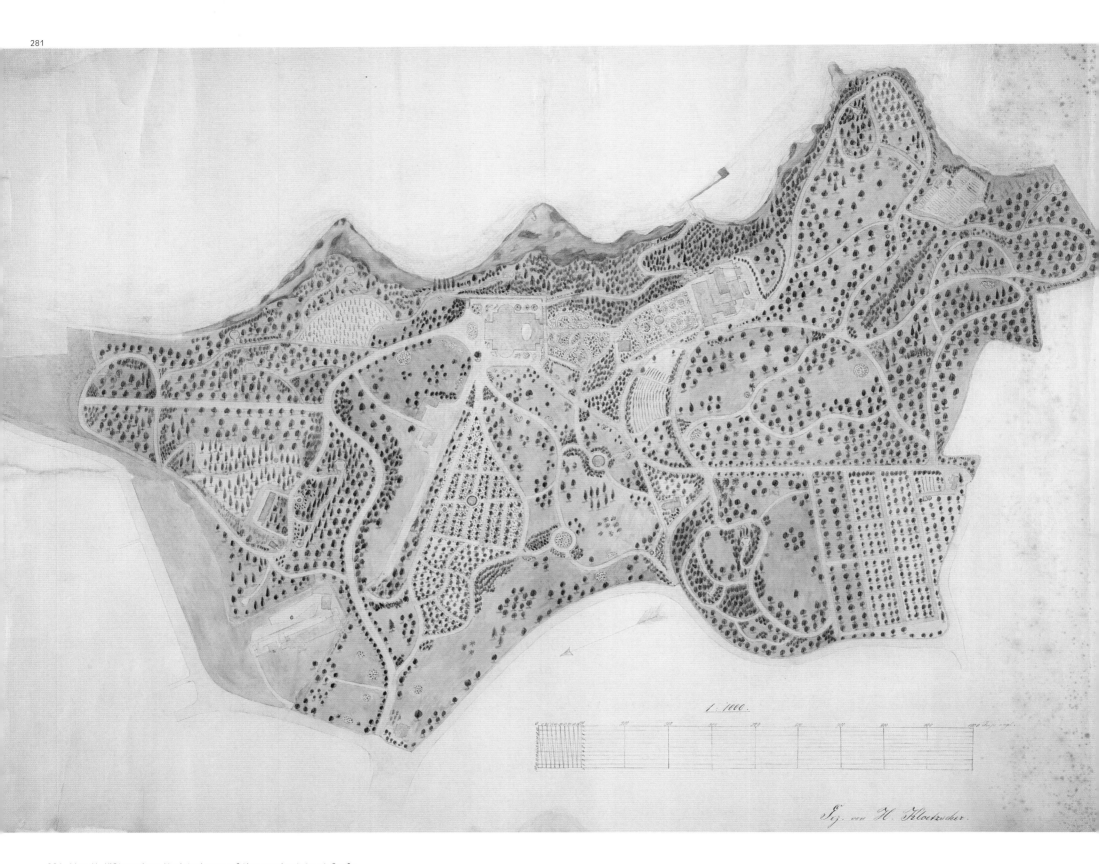

1 : 1000.

*Sig. von H. Klötzscher.*

**281.** *Von H. Klötzscher. Undated map of the royal estate at Corfu from the late 19th century (1882?). National Historical Museum.*

# CORFU

## MON REPOS

**M**on Repos stands in the centre of a large 23.8 hectare park on Corfu's Kanoni peninsula.

The villa was built on Agios Panteleimon hill at public expense by Sir Frederick Adam when he took over from Sir Thomas Maitland as Lord High Commissioner of the island, which was a British protectorate between 1815 and 1864, in 1824. Adam had lived on Corfu since 1821 as governor of the Ionian islands, during which time he met and fell in love with a young Corfiote aristocrat, Nina (Diamantina) Palatianou, who helped hone his philhellene sentiments and is said to have persuaded her husband to build the villa, which belonged to the state. Work began in 1828 and was completed in 1831.

The architect is not known. Sissy Kyriaki, who has studied the villa in detail, believes it was probably the work of the well-known Corfiote architect, Ioannis Chronis, though Sir George Whitmore, an engineer with the British Royal Engineers, or a group of other British military engineers, cannot be ruled out. However, Chronis had just returned to Corfu in 1821 after completing his studies, and it seems unlikely that the Lord High Commissioner would assign the design of his personal residence to an inexperienced, albeit talented, young man. On the other hand, there is evidence that Sir Frederick Adam particularly admired Chronis' work, though this was a few years later when the latter had demonstrated his architectural abilities in practice and Adam employed him to design his second country residence: Chryseis. This makes Sir George Whitmore or a group of four engineers the most probable creators, though the former makes no mention of the villa in his memoirs.

Adam was the grandson and great nephew respectively of three of England's most important 18th-century architects: John, James and Robert Adam, the last of whom is considered the link between English Palladianism and the Romantic, Classical and Gothic styles of the 19th century; there can be no doubt he would

**282.** *Mon Repos in the early 20th century. Benaki Museum.*

**283.** *The same view in colour, from a period postcard.*

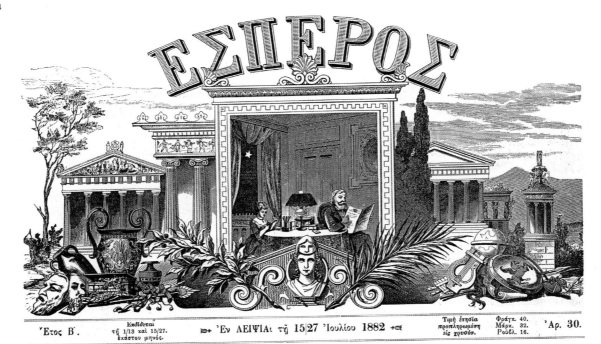

ΕΣΠΕΡΟΣ

Ἔτος Β΄. | Ἐκδίδεται τῇ 1/13 καὶ 15/27. ἑκάστου μηνός. | ⇒• Ἐν ΛΕΙΨΙΑι τῇ 15|27 Ἰουλίου 1882 •⇐ | Τιμὴ ἐτησία προπληρωμένη εἰς χρυσόν. | Φράγκ. 40. Μάρκ. 32. Ρούβλ. 16. | Ἀρ. 30.

Η ΒΑΣΙΛΙΚΗ ΕΠΑΥΛΙΣ ΕΝ ΚΕΡΚΥΡΑι.

have had his own views on the form of his personal residence. Moreover, all military men had some knowledge of architecture at this time, since it was a required subject in military schools across Europe (including the Cadet School in Nafplion, newly founded by Kapodistrias). It is not impossible, therefore, that he drew up a preliminary design for the villa himself, or asked for a design to be sent from England for him to use as a model.

Villas of this type featured in architectural handbooks of the 18th and early 19th centuries, and it is quite possible that Whitmore or Kyriaki's group of four simply undertook to localize the design and oversee the construction of the building, as was common practice at the time. An examination of the Adam family archive could well shed further light on the subject.

The villa, which Adam named "Casino", was widely commented on at the time; its completion was marked by a grand ball staged in the villa in the last week of 1831.

A villa in the English neoclassical style, its ground floor housed reception rooms and its first floor, which was reached by way of a wide central wooden staircase, was given over to the bedrooms and private sitting rooms. The principle of symmetry was strictly observed both in the ground plan and on the building's original façades. The main entrance, which is emphasised by a Doric porch and a pair of lamp-stands on either side of the porch, is in the centre of the villa's north-eastern aspect. The central section of the upper storey, which corresponds to the first-floor sitting room, projects slightly forward and gives onto the balcony above the entrance porch; the ground floor features two small semicircular projections at the ends of the villa enclosed by two porticos, also semicircular, facing the garden. These porticos are connected with sitting rooms on the ground floor by large French doors to create the pleasant verandas that are essential in any Mediterranean country. The porticos were topped by semicircular balconies on the upper floor.

It is worth quoting at this point the description of the interior by L.C. Ippoviz, seeing as it is our only description of the inside of the building in the 19th and early 20th century.

285

ΚΕΡΚΥΡΑ — ΒΑΣΙΛΙΚΗ ΕΠΑΥΛΙΣ   CORFOU — VILLA ROYALE DE
           "MON REPOS"                          "MON REPOS"

"Ἔκδοσις τῆς Ἑλληνικῆς ταχυδρομικῆς ὑπηρεσίας".
«Edition du service des Postes Helléniques».

284. *Mon Repos, from the* Esperos *newspaper, 1882.*

285. *Mon Repos. Postcard. Published by the Hellenic Postal Service.*

Pages 222-223

286. *Mon Repos. View from the SW.*

"One enters the villa from the east by way of a gentle flight of steps flanked by marble lamp-stands [...]. The peristyle consists of somewhat short, fat columns which successfully imitate the antique and leads to the elegant staircase which is well-lit and abloom with flowers, adorned with chandeliers and a large oil painting depicting a scene from the *Odyssey* [...]. Turning right in the hall, one finds oneself in the billiard room, which is done out in green. Next come the bedrooms, all of which are similar and appointed, in the main, in pastel shades with light-hued wooden furniture imported from Paris. The walls are decorated with a variety of fine, modern motifs which the royal family brought back only this year. The oval-shaped breakfast room is to the left of the peristyle and furnished with elegant dark antique furniture and dark curtains [...]. One then comes to other rooms set aside for work and slumber. The floors of all these rooms, and those on the first floor, are covered with soft, well-kept carpets.

Ascending the staircase, one comes to the first-floor colonnade, which is capped by a dome. It is my belief that this is the finest space in the building, architecturally-speaking [...]. The side niches contain light-fittings [...] which were purchased, along with a statue, from the Paris Exhibition of 1889. Turning left, one enters the king's salon, whose furniture is all carved [...]. The view of the sea from this room is breath-taking. The room interconnects with the queen's salon. The paintings include two works by Prosalentis [...]. It should be added that all the rooms and chambers are adorned with exceedingly fine marble fireplaces in a range of styles, as is the custom in English country houses. From the king's salon, we proceed into the queen's study, whose walls are covered with water-colours depicting the most beautiful parts of the island [...]. One can go out onto the balcony from the study and enjoy the exquisite views over the city. This is followed by the king's work room, whose furniture and walls are lined with gold-trimmed leather [...]. From here, one can enter the smoking room, which is done out in dark red and whose walls, in addition to the modern printed motifs, are adorned with fine water-colours by Roberti, a 'Maddalena' by Prosalentis and works by other artists [...]. From here, one enters the young princes' large, carpeted study [...]. The view from the window is entirely different

**287.** *Mon Repos. Detail of the northern elevation.*

**288.** *Mon Repos. The villa from the south.*

Pages 226-227

**289.** *Mon Repos. The semi-circular projection on the eastern elevation and the belvedere's balustrade.*

from the vista visible from the balcony, which looks over a large tranquil park [...]. From here, traversing the colonnade, one can enter the queen's austere bed chamber [...] which features a fine fireplace with bronze divinities. Next in line is the 'tavoletta' [...] from which can enter the park directly. The king's bed chamber is on the opposite side, and is no less plain and unassuming than that of the queen. Its walls are decorated with elegant modern stamps depicting mythological creatures...".

The most characteristic feature of the villa is the wonderful garden in which it is set. It is an English-style, informal garden with shady retreats, small glades, winding paths and ancient ruins which matched the aesthetic of the English garden and imbued it with style and a picturesque quality. The variety of trees (cedars, maples and sarsaparilla), many of which were imported especially from England, shrubs, ornamental plants and flowers evoked the admiration of visitors to the park, which is said to have contained some 2,000 plant and tree species.

Later, when Elisabeth of Austria was a house guest of the British High Commissioner in Mon Repos, she wrote in her diary that the garden spread out before the villa "as though leaves and flowers are spilling from a cornucopia into the sea; the aloes and palm trees raise their ethereal heads towards the blue sky and golden oranges gleam like stars amongst the shady vegetation. Consul Warsberg used to say that it was the garden of Alkinoos".

Baron Pierre de Coubertin, whose name is inextricably linked with the revival of the Olympic Games, compared Mon Repos' grounds with the Garden of Eden, and commented on the outstanding view over the gulf of Garitsa, the town and the Albanian coast opposite. On the eastern side of the villa, there is an equally wonderful view over the boundless sea.

Adam enjoyed his country villa on Corfu for only four years. In 1832, he was assigned to India as governor of Madras. His successor, Lord Nugent, lived in the palace of Saints Michael and George in Corfu town, a building constructed by Whitmore in 1819-1824 as the residence of the Lord High Commissioner of the

Pages 228-229
290. *Mon Repos. The porch on the northern elevation.*

291. *Mon Repos. The lamp-stand before the porch.*

292. *Mon Repos. The base of the porch lamp-stand. It bears two inscriptions: "Ch. Siegel in Athen Fecit" and "Χ. Ε. Σείγγελος Αθηναίος εποίησεν" [C.E. Singelos, an Athenian, made this].*

293. *Unsigned plan for the Mon Repos stables. National Historical Museum.*

294. *R. Hubert. Drawings for the Mon Repos stables. 1891. National Historical Museum.*

293

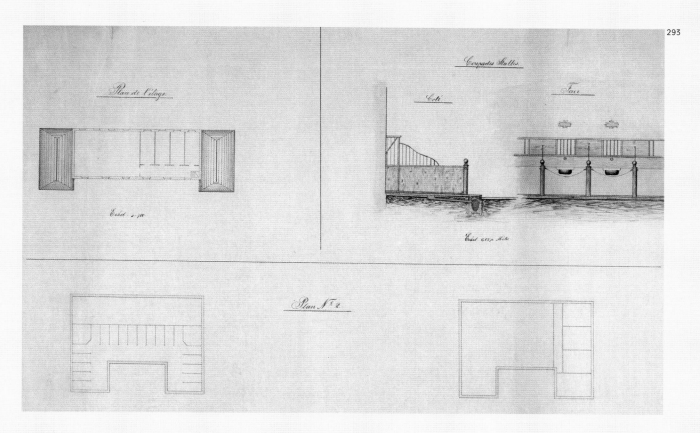

294

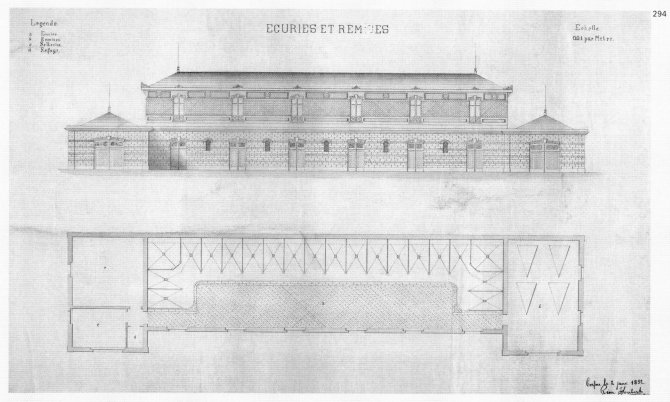

ECURIES ET REMISES

231

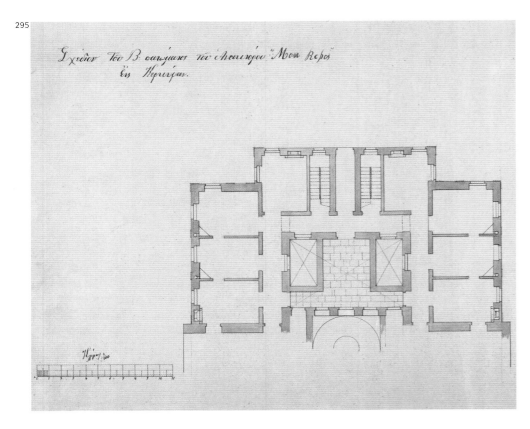

295-297. *Mon Repos. Plans for the mansion's expansion to the rear. Plans for first floor, second floor and the roof. National Historical Museum.*

298. *Mon Repos. View from the terrace.*

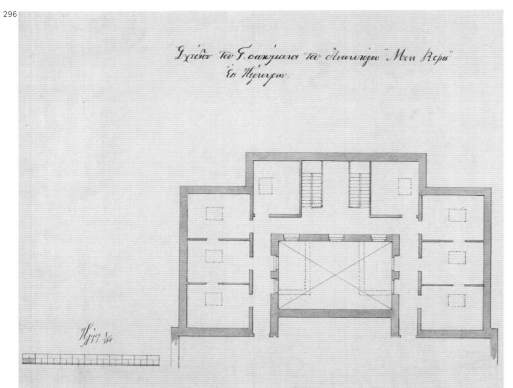

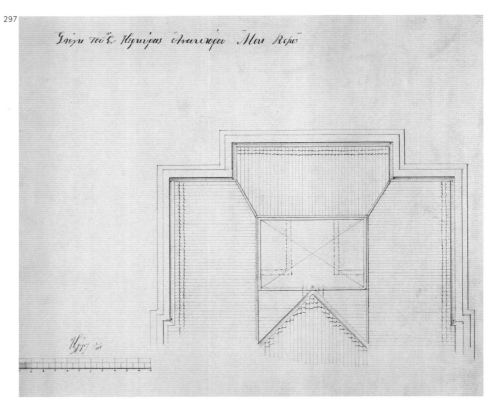

**299.** *Mon Repos. The ornate octagonal drum of the dome.*

**300.** *Mon Repos. The main octagonal room on the first floor. The Ionic columns support a richly decorated entablature with a frieze featuring rosettes and other plant motifs and a cornice with modillions. Similar decorations exist on the base of the drum.*

Ionian islands and Grand Master of the Order of the Knights of Saints Michael and George. The building also housed the Legislative Assembly and the Ionian Senate.

Mon Repos or Casino was made over to the Senate for "the common good" with the recommendation that it should house the Ionian Academy and that its gardens should be used as a place of recreation by the good citizens of Corfu. Although later proposals included its conversion into an art museum, a School of Fine Arts, a school of Agronomy and a seminary, it ultimately served as a museum and School of Fine Arts for a long period, while the attic rooms were used as the residence of the director of the school, P. Prosalentis, and his family. In 1834, the School of Fine Arts was transferred to the town, and on the suggestion of the fourth Lord High Commissioner, Sir Howard Douglas, the seminary was housed in the palace for a short time (1840-42). In the years that followed, it was occasionally used by the Lords High Commissioner as a summer residence for brief periods.

In 1861, it was made available for four months to the empress Elisabeth (Sissi) of Austria on her first visit to Corfu. This visit led, thirty years later, to her buying a private property on the island on which she built her own palace: the Achilleion.

After the unification of the Ionian islands with Greece in 1864, the island's provisional council made a gift of the villa and the park around it to the young king George to use as a summer residence. It was probably at this time that it acquired the name Mon Repos, the name by which it is known today. Enraptured by this wonderful area, George bought small parcels of land from time to time which, coupled with small plots of land presented to him by various neighbours, boosted the size of the estate considerably until it acquired its current form and was recorded as the personal property of the king in the Corfu land registry in December 1882.

George bequeathed the area in his handwritten will to his son, Prince Andrew, father of Prince Philip of England, who sold it to George II. It was then bequeathed first to King Paul and then to his heir: Constantine II.

When it was in use as a palace, the ground floor housed the dining and sitting rooms, the king's study and his adjutant's office; the rear was given over to the kitchen, central heating installations and ancillary rooms. The first floor housed the royal bedrooms, and the upper gallery the guest quarters.

301

301. *Mon Repos. The room with a semi-circular side on the ground-floor (now the billiard room). The white and pink floor tiles can be made out. On the right, a full-length painting of Lady Adam.*

George's archives contain a series of drawings of the estate and the villa– which is why the villa came to be included in this volume despite predating the arrival of the Glücksberg dynasty in Greece.

The earliest of these documents, a map of the estate, is undated and unsigned, though a comparison with a similar map of Agios Panteleimon made in 1864, which is now in the Corfu Prefectural Archives, places it a few years later than this; it was probably done in 1882, after the addition of the new facilities. The estate gardens are clearly marked with their winding paths and areas of crops, as is the small house belonging to Justice Colholme, the island's British judge, with its separate entrance in the north-west corner of the estate, the Monastery of Agia Evfimia and a number of outhouses.

The other six drawings, also unsigned and undated, relate to the rear extension of the villa. The style of the drawing and the handwriting used would indicate that they are contemporaneous with those depicting the ancillary buildings at Tatoi, meaning that they date from the early 20th century and the reign of George I (since they were part of the museum dedicated to that monarch).

The first, entitled "Diagram of the Second building of Mon Repos on Corfu", depicts the connection between the villa's outhouses (stables, kitchen, etc.) and its main water supply. The ground plan of the extension's ground floor is included to the rear of the villa.

The next five drawings contain two slightly different versions of the ground plan of the first and second floors, and one of the roof.

**302.** *Mon Repos. A first storey hall with a semi-circular side (the king's drawing room).*

303

**303.** *Mon Repos. The room facing east, with a semi-circular side (breakfast room). On the left, a white marble fireplace.*

**304.** *Mon Repos. The main staircase. The steps are made of solid stone; the banister in the shape of a double helix is wrought iron with a wooden hand-rail.*

Ippovitz's description of the building from 1902 notes that: "it has a ground floor and upper storey, and the overall structure is vaulted", and that it has thirty-five rooms in all. As Kyriaki has observed, this description is of the original villa plus the ground-floor extension, which must therefore have been added before Ippoviz's visit. This accounts for there being no detailed plans of the ground floor in the afore-mentioned series of drawings, since it already existed.

The drawings make it clear that the extension was to be used for bedrooms on the upper storey and ancillary rooms on the ground floor. The existence of a large number of bedrooms confirms that it was designed during the reign of George I or in the first years of the reign of Constantine I, since the families of

both were in need of several bedrooms (George had seven children and Constantine six). It is not impossible that the upper-storey extension was designed in 1908, when Kaiser Wilhelm II of Germany, Princess Sophia's brother, bought the Achilleion from Franz-Joseph and his daughter Valeria, and commissioned Ziller to build a new wing so he could holiday on Corfu. The Kaiser's decision may have stirred the Greek royal family into action.

The king's plans were probably interrupted by the Balkan Wars, the Asia Minor Disaster and other epoch-making events. After George I's death in 1913, the estate was the property of Prince Andrew until 1937; it was here that his son, Philip, was born in 1921.

Two more drawings in the same group depict stables. One is dated January 1892 and signed 'P. Aubust', the other is unsigned and undated. The morphology of Aubust's stables is more elaborate in the picturesque manner. The central section of his stables has two storeys, and probably housed the head groom's quarters; the central part of the second proposal also has two storeys, though it is much simpler.

The present form of the villa is not very different from that designed by the island's chief engineer, A. Ortentsatos, in 1936, which was based on the earlier drawings described above. It is not known when the second storey envisioned in plans drawn up by I. Kollas in 1955 was added to the central body of the building. The royal family are known to have made a number of modifications and repairs to the building before the Second World War, but we do not know precisely what these were. Additional modifications and repairs designed to bring the building up to date were made in 1955 by Kollas himself, who also built the Tito pavilion at the back of the villa for the President of Yugoslavia.

The villa and estate now belong to the Municipality of Corfu; the building is to be turned into a museum, its estate into a public garden.

**305.** *Mon Repos. Detail of the first storey balcony.*

**306.** *Mon Repos. The portrait of Sir Frederic Adam above his desk in the red room on the ground floor.*

# THE PALACE OF SAINTS MICHAEL AND GEORGE

**T**his palace and the Achilleion are special cases. Both were built by foreigners, the former by the British High Commissioner of the Ionian islands and the latter as a summer residence for Empress Elisabeth of Austria. However, since they were built on Greek soil during the 19th century, they fall within the ambit of this work and will be briefly discussed here.

The palace of Saints Michael and George was built between 1814 and 1824 on the north side of the Spianada, Corfu Town's central square. Constructed during the period of British rule (the island was a British protectorate, 1814-1864), it is in the Georgian neoclassical style which developed in England during the 19th and early 20th century and whose main exponent was Robert Adam. The palace was commissioned by the first Lord High Commissioner of the Ionian islands, Sir

307. C. Whitmore. The palace of Saints Michael and George.

308. The palace of Saints Michael and George. The auxiliary side wing.

309

Thomas Maitland, to serve as his residence. Until then, the Venetian *Provveditore* had lived in the Old Fort of Corfu. During the island's French period (1807-1814), a hospital stood on the site on which the palace was later built.

The building was designed and built by Sir George Whitmore (1775-1862), a graduate of the British Royal Military Academy, who was serving in Corfu as a colonel. It was at this time that the two most important buildings on the island were designed: the palace of Saints Michael and George and the circular pavilion on the Spianada known as Maitland's Rotunda in honour of the first Lord High Commissioner.

The central part of the palace has three storeys and a U-shaped ground plan facing onto an internal courtyard. A long portico in front of the building on the side giving onto the Spianada links it with two side wings at a ground-floor level by way of two arches bearing the names of Saints Michael and George respectively.

This long prostyle portico has 32 Doric columns on pedestals which, the island *Gazzetta* informs us, were modelled on the columns of the Parthenon. The arcade curves into a semicircle where it meets the side wings. The three official rooms on the upper storey open onto a large balcony above the portico.

The façade of the building is plain and austere, the only decoration on the central crowning being the carved symbols of the seven Ionian islands in relief with Britannia above them in the centre holding a horn of plenty. The work of the Maltese sculptor, Dimech, their execution was supervised by Pavlos Prosalentis. The statue of Britannia was removed after the unification of the Ionian islands with Greece and replaced by the prow of a Corfiote trireme carved in stone.

**309.** *The palace of Saints Michael and George. Detail of the front elevation.*

The main entrance hall is surrounded by a slightly raised passageway. The bases of the Ionic columns in the hall's internal colonnade were modelled on the bases from the temple of Athena Polias at Priene. The internal peristyle is crowned by a frieze with panels containing scenes from the Odyssey and leads to the Assembly and Senate rooms.

A large central staircase at the end of the hall leads up to the first-floor antechamber whose dome is supported on eight columns, replicas of those on the Lysicrates Monument in Athens. The three large reception rooms are directly opposite and connect, as noted above, with the gallery from which there is a superb view over the Spianada.

The main ballroom is circular and has a coffered ceiling and a parquet floor of oak, olive, chestnut and mahogany. The walls around it are adorned with mirrors, and there are four niches containing female statues in the corners of the square encasing the circular space. The room named after Saint Michael was used as a dining room; Saint George's room opposite served as a throne room, while the members of the Knights of the Order of Michael and George, which was founded in 1818 so the relevant honours could be awarded to occupants of Ionian islands and Malta, were proclaimed in both. The wings behind the two legs of the U served as the High Commissioner's official residence; the royal family of Greece stayed there occasionally between Corfu's incorporation into the Greek state and World War Two. A statue of Frederick Adam by Prosalentis stands in front of the building, in the centre of a small fountain.

In 1994, the palace served as the venue for the EU summit during the Greek presidency, and hosted the twelve leaders of the member states at the time.

310

310. *Pavlos Prosalentis. Statue of Fr. Adam.*

**311-314.** *The Achilleion, when it was being used as an imperial mansion by Kaiser Wilhelm II of Germany. Benaki Museum, Photographic Archive.*

# THE ACHILLEION

In May 1861, empress Elisabeth (Sissi) of Austria visited Corfu for the first time at the age of twenty-four. She was enchanted by the island and returned a month later to stay in Mon Repos with the British Lord High Commissioner. On one of her carriage tours of the island, she called in at Gastouri and came to know the estate of Petros Vrailas-Armenis. The empress would visit Corfu on at least another three occasions over the next twenty-eight years, and it was on one of her visits, during which she was a guest at Vrailas' country house, that she decided to purchase the estate and build a palace there.

As Elisabeth puts it: "I dedicated my palace to the dying Achilles, since for me he represents the Greek soul and the beauty of the land and the people [...]. He was strong and proud [...]. He held nothing sacred or holy besides his own will and he lived his dreams: for him, his grief was more precious than the whole of life…".

The palace was built to designs by the Austrian consul, Alexander von Warsberg, by the Italian architects Raffaele Caritto and Antonio Landi under the supervision of August von Bucovick. The empress herself, who had just lost her only son Rudolph, took a great interest in its construction, travelling frequently to the island and taking a personal interest in the decoration of the palace and the garden. Indeed, she elected to place her son's cenotaph in a tranquil corner of the latter; emperor Franz-Joseph had the monument transferred to Vienna after Elisabeth's death.

The palace is a highly eclectic three-storey, neoclassical building with a rectangular plan. Open and covered balconies, terraces, porticos and colonnades, pavilions, pergolas and belvedere terraces form a complex in which interior, open air spaces and verandas are interchanged to create the islands of tranquillity and solitude that Elisabeth wanted.

She would awake at five every morning and walk alone through her hanging gardens, surrounded by magnolias, cypresses and oleanders. From on high, the

315a

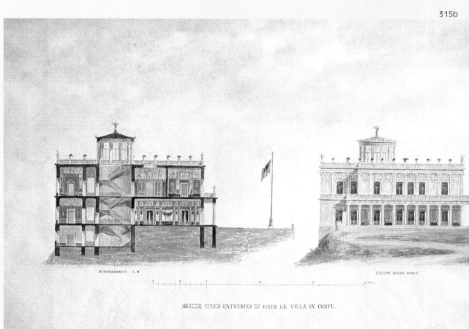

315b

315. T. Hansen. Proposal for a mansion on Corfu for the empress Elisabeth.
a. Façade, b. Longitudinal section and side elevation.

town and harbour of Corfu could be seen in the distance, with the endless blue of the sea in the background.

In the interior of the building, the neoclassical style interacted with the Pompeian, the Baroque and even the Rococo in the palace's wall and ceiling paintings and tumult of sculpted decoration, which was not always in the best taste. The interior decoration was the work of the Italian artists Palioti, Bostiglioni and Scami, who adorned the palace rooms and garden with an abundance of paintings and sculptures connected, in the main, with Achilles, the hero so beloved by the empress, and other heroes of Greek mythology. Most of the sculptures were purchased from Prince Borghese.

The ground floor housed the reception rooms and a room designed as a Catholic chapel on whose wall an oil painting depicted the Virgin extending her hand protectively above the imperial yacht *Miramare*, which had recently come through a terrible storm at sea unharmed. The statue of Notre Dame de la Garde, the patron saint of French sailors presented to Elisabeth in Marseilles, stood behind the sanctuary to the right.

A grand staircase began in the entrance hall, dividing into a double staircase on the first landing and leading up to the upper storeys where the other reception rooms and the empress's personal quarters were to be found.

The villa and the garden recall the opulence of a Roman villa. The artists whose work adorned the Achilleion include the painters Franz Winterhalter, Sobeslav Pinkas and Ludwig Thierch and the sculptors Antonio Canova and Ernst Herter, while there were also a large number of contemporary copies of ancient busts

**316, 317.** *The Achilleion. General views. Benaki Museum, Photographic Archive.*

**318.** *The Achilleion.* The Leaping wrestlers, *at the end of the colonnade on the rear verandah. In the background, the statues of* Dying Achilles *and* Resting Hermes. *Benaki Museum, Photographic Archive.*

**319.** *The Achilleion. View of the garden toward the peristyle. Benaki Museum, Photographic Archive.*

**320, 321.** *The Achilleion. View of the garden. Benaki Museum, Photographic Archive.*

318 319

320 321

247

Palais Imperial

of ancient Greek philosophers, orators and poets, as well as a bust of Shakespeare. The most important sculpture in the imperial villa, however, is undoubtedly the *Dying Achilles* by Ernst Herter which took pride of place in the garden. It was a copy of a smaller sculpture that adorned Elisabeth's Villa Hermes in Vienna. The second most important statue in the Achilleion was that of the great poet and writer Heinrich Heine whose work was greatly admired by Elisabeth; the statue by the Danish sculptor Hasselrüs depicts Heine sitting in his armchair and stood in a small round pavilion.

The Achilleion was used by Elisabeth as a retreat, and she spent a large part of her latter years there until she was assassinated by an Italian anarchist in 1898.

For about ten years the villa and estate lay empty. In spring 1905, Kaiser Wilhelm II of Germany, the brother of Princess Sophia, visited Corfu at the invitation of the Greek royal family. He visited the Achilleion, was impressed and purchased the estate shortly afterwards (1907) from emperor Franz Joseph and his daughter Valeria (Gisela), the wife of Leopold von Bayern.

It was at this time that the House of the Knights was built in the western part of the garden, to the left of the large iron gates leading into the estate, to provide quarters for the Kaiser's staff. One of Ernst Ziller's last projects, it helped the architect recover from the financial problems that had beset him since the bankruptcy of the Greek state had left him without commissions for a considerable length of time. Early in July 1907, Ziller left for Berlin to submit his designs and budget for the House of Knights to the Kaiser and his court architect. The meeting was also attended by Raffaelo Caritto, the architect who had designed the Achilleion. His plans approved, Ziller returned to Greece and completed the new building, which had forty rooms, in only six months, overseeing the decoration in person while carrying out repairs and modifications on the main building. Ziller was decorated by Wilhelm II for his efforts.

Having moved into the Achilleion, Wilhelm erected a huge 5.5 m. high statue of *Achilles Victorious* by the German sculptor Johannes Götz on the large terrace on the spot previously occupied by the statue of *Dying Achilles*, which he had moved to the middle terrace. Wilhelm's statue originally bore the inscription: "Erected to Achilles, son of Peleus, by Wilhelm of the Mighty Germans, in memoriam". He also replaced the statue of Heine in the small marble pavilion with a statue of Elisabeth herself, so that her memory would be kept alive

**322, 323.** *The Achilleion. Steps leading from the terraces to the garden. Benaki Museum, Photographic Archive.*

**324.** *The Achilleion. The* Leaping wrestlers. *Colonnade, rear verandah.*

**325.** *The Achilleion. Part of the front elevation. The bronze statues of two Hestias are visible above the richly-ornamented first-storey verandah; the statue of Winged Hermes is in the background. Benaki Museum, Photographic Archive.*

**326.** *The Achilleion. Leda and the Swan. Benaki Museum, Photographic Archive.*

**327.** *The Achilleion. The Dying Achilles, by Ernst Herter. Benaki Museum, Photographic Archive.*

**328, 329.** *The Achilleion. The peristyle of the Muses during the building's Kaiser Wilhelm period. Benaki Museum, Photographic Archive.*

330 331

**330.** *The Achilleion. The main entrance. On the left, a relief depiction of Achilles in his chariot.*

**331.** *The Achilleion. Detail of a ground-floor window.*

**332.** *The Achilleion. Side elevation.*

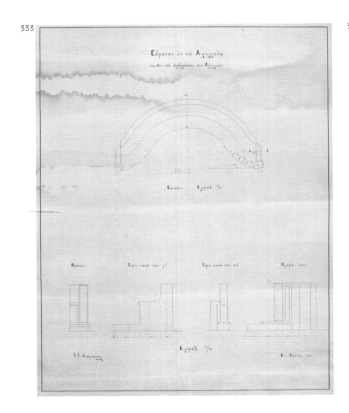

333

334

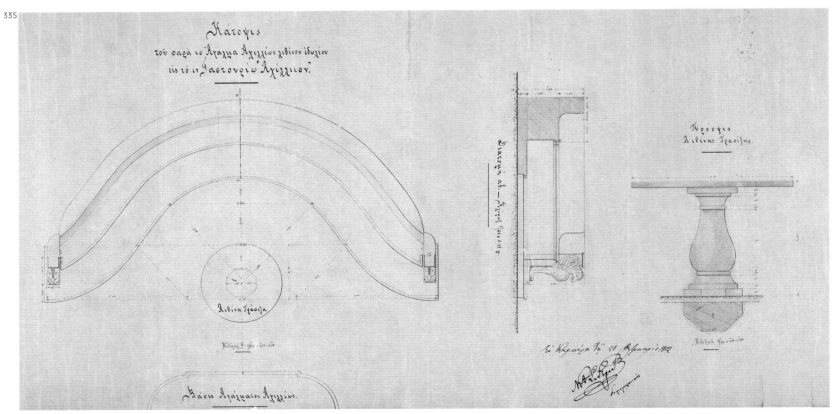

335

on the estate she had created. The statue is now in the Murillon gardens in Toulon, France.

The house was refurnished by Prechtel of Berlin, purveyors of traditional furniture, in a style appropriate both to the palace and to a summer house. Some of the rooms had wicker furniture that could also be used in the garden.

The Kaiser visited the Achilleion over a period of six years, during which time the villa played host to many leading figures including royalty, politicians, archaeologists (Wilhelm took a personal interest in the excavations being conducted on the island at that time) and men and women of the arts and letters. In his memoirs, the Kaiser describes the garden and the estate in detail, as well as his family's hasty departure from the island when war was declared in the spring of 1914: "We left behind a whole world", he writes "and that world was beautiful".

In 1919, the Achilleion became the property of the Greek state. It now belongs to the Greek National Tourist Organisation and houses Corfu's casino; there is a small museum devoted to the history of the building, with artefacts associated with Elisabeth and Wilhelm, on the ground floor.

336

337

333. *The Achilleion. Garden bench (detail). National Historical Museum.*

334. *The Achilleion. Marble bench.*

335. *The Achilleion. Design for a stone pedestal and table for the* Dying Achilles *terrace. National Historical Museum.*

336. *The Achilleion. The entrance hall as it is today. The ceiling decoration is the work of the Italian painter Gallopi.*

337. *The Achilleion. The entrance hall and main staircase in the time of Kaiser Wilhelm. Benaki Museum, Photographic Archive.*

**338.** *The Achilleion. Achilles' Triumph,* a work by the Austrian painter Franz von März, *on the second landing leading up to the upper storey.*

**339.** *The Achilleion. The main staircase. Sculpted figures from Greek mythology flank the intricate wrought-iron banister with the wooden hand rail.*

Palais Imperial

**340.** *The Achilleion. Empress Elisabeth's dining room.*
*Benaki Museum, Photographic Archive.*

**341.** *The Achilleion. Detail from a fireplace in Elisabeth's dining room.*
*An oil painting by the Bavarian painter Ludwig Tiersch depicting* Ulysses
*and* Nausica *hangs over the mantelpiece.*

**342.** *The Achilleion. Elisabeth's chapel, dedicated to the Stella del Mare. The ceiling of the dome above*
*the sanctuary depicts Jesus in the Praetorium. Statues of Christ and the Virgin Mary by Franz von März*
*stand in the niches flanking the icon of the Stella del Mare.*

**343**. *The Achilleion. The view from the belvedere.*

**344**. *The Achilleion. Marble statues flanking the Staircase of the Gods: Apollo on the right, Hermes on the left.*

345

345, 346. *The Achilleion. Views of the garden.*

347. *The Achilleion. The terrace on which the* Dying Achilles *stands.*

346

# ROYAL RESIDENCES ELSEWHERE IN GREECE

A number of other buildings that were used as residences by the royal couple or the princes in the 19th and early 20th century were temporarily designated palaces. They include the Palace of the Lord of Samos at Vathy and the Palace of Prince George (the High Commissioner of Crete, 1898-1906) at Rethymnon (which now houses the offices of the Prefecture).

Buildings in Athens referred to as palaces at the end of the 19th century include the Negreponte-Louriotis Residence (now demolished), in which the heir to the throne lived until the palace in Irodou Attikou Street was complete; the Psychas Mansion on Vasilissis Sophias Avenue, where prince Nicholas lived; the villas occupied by Paul and Frederica as heirs to the throne; princess Eleni's residence in Psychiko; and the villa belonging to the Duchess of Plaisance in which Constantine II lived as heir to the throne.

In Thessaloniki, too, a series of private residences were used by kings or princes and dubbed 'palaces'. We could mention the Francis Charnaud (subsequently

**348.** *Samos. The Sovereign's palace.*

**349.** *Chania. The Commissioner's palace.*

**350.** *Rethymnon. The Commissioner's palace. Postcard.*

**351.** *Athens. The Negreponte-Louriotis Residence in Amalia St. Designed by E. Troump. Benaki Museum, Neohellenic Architecture Archive.*

*e Palais du Prince à la Canée.*

Chatzilazaros) Mansion, where king George I lived 1912-1913, which features in a postcard of the time encaptioned "the entrance to the palace (Ch. Lazaros villa) of the national martyr King George I in Thessaloniki"; an additional Chatzilazaros residence which served as a palace for the Crown Prince during the same period; the Modiano residence (now the city's Folklore Museum), which was made available to King Constantine I to serve as a palace between the death of George I and 1916; and the Periklis Chatzilazaros Villa, which seems to have accommodated other members of the royal family between 1912 and 1913.

Finally, in the mid 20th century (1960), the architect Periklis Sakellarios built a striking building in the neoclassical style on Thessaloniki's Karabounaki promontory to serve as a government office and a residence for the members of the royal family and other VIPs who visited Greece's second city; the building was quickly dubbed the "little palace". With the exception of this latter building, however, all of Thessaloniki's 'palaces' were actually grand bourgeois mansions and villas where members of the royal family were entertained for short periods of time and to which no changes or additions were made as a result, or in view of, their royal service. They therefore have no place in this volume.

**352.** *The Periklis Chatzilazaros residence.*
*Used as a palace by the princes.*

**353.** *The M. Kapantzis residence.*
*Used as a palace by Prince Nikolaos.*

**354.** *The Modiano residence.*
*Used as a palace by King Constantine.*

**355.** *The Hadji Agiah residence.*
*Used as a palace by the Crown Prince.*
*Postcards.*

# EPILOGUE

The 19th was the last century –for the foreseeable future, at least– in which kings ruled men by "divine right", even if they had lost much of the power they wielded in early eras.

Still, the enormous political, social and ideological changes that followed in the wake of the French Revolution did not prevent Napoleon from proclaiming himself emperor or his generals from being called kings; indeed, the present king of Norway is descended from one of Bonaparte's commanders.

Nor did the awakening of the subjugated nationalities that began to struggle for their emancipation obliterate the allure of the monarchy; why else, after a century of bloody rebellions which finally secured the –albeit conditional– liberation of Greece from the Ottoman yoke, would Hellas hasten to despatch her heroes to kneel before an immature youth, a mere child, and offer him her crown, just a few months after the Greek governor of the Greek Republic was assassinated to satisfy the demands of a vendetta? This is neither the time nor the place to engage in a more profound analysis of these themes, or to sketch connections and associations with the policies being pursued across Europe during this period of instability and change. Analysis of this kind, in any case, is the task of historians, not architects.

During the period under consideration, in which states multiplied across Europe and the institution of the –constitutional– monarchy remained stable, the new kings in Bavaria, Prussia, Saxony, Austria, Denmark, Sweden and elsewhere chose to consolidate their authority by building palaces.

The dream of every self-respecting architect who wished to make a name for himself internationally was to build at least one palace, if not for a king, than for at least a prince, duke or count.

The newly-formed Greek state was an attractive proposition on two counts: firstly, because the conditions preceding its foundation had not been conducive to the creation of similar buildings for at least four centuries, and secondly, because the international preoccupation with the ancient Greek roots of the arts and philosophy had placed the country at the epicentre of the interests of every cultivated European humanist. Indeed, Greece had already emerged as a place of pilgrimage for archaeologists and architects during the 18th century, when neoclassicism came to dominate architecture in Europe and had even reached America's far-flung shores.

A palace in Greece, a neoclassical palace – what more could an architect wish for? Particularly when the young king was the son of Ludwig of Bavaria, a man whose philhellenism and passion for Greece were unprecedented and have not, indeed, been matched since.

Schinkel, Lange, Klenze, Christian and Theophilus Hansen, all of them great architects of the day, dreamed of building a Greek palace. Ziller was a slightly different case: he appeared on the scene a few years later, when neoclassicism was in decline and, being personally acquainted with the new king, George I, proposed designs which he believed would accord with the monarch's personal tastes – though they were grandiose, impressive designs nonetheless.

Why none of the Greek architects of the period, including the two leading lights of Greek architecture, Stamatis Kleanthis and Lysandros Kaftantzoglou, ever attempted to design a palace is puzzling. Did they lack confidence in their ability? Did they believe that the foreign monarch would never commission a palace from a Greek? Or were they motivated by purely ideological factors? We do not know. The only two who turned their attention to the subject, albeit for a short time, were Gerasimos and Anastasis Metaxas, architects of the royal court, though the palace they designed for the king at Tripoli was really a summer villa rather than a palace in the full sense of the word.

Nevertheless, none of Greece's palaces, with the possible exception of Gärtner's, could match the scale of their counterparts in Great Britain, France, Germany and the rest of Europe. The finances of the newly-founded Greek state could not stretch to the expense such a building would entail, and it did not take long for the first Greek monarch to grasp this reality. The loan Ludwig of Bavaria made available to build the palace was actually derived from the "French defence budget" granted by France to Bavaria to erect fortresses along her western frontiers, and thus had to be repaid both rapidly and in large instalments. Not surprisingly, the debt became insupportable, particularly after Ludwig abdicated in 1848 and was succeeded by Maximilian, who failed to persuade the Bavarian parliament to moderate its demands. For his part, Otto could not muster the resources required to pay even the interest on the loan to Bavaria; the debt was eventually settled several years after his expulsion.

Thus, even though George I dearly wanted to build new summer palaces in the provinces, he wisely restricted his demands. It helped that he was, in any case, a plain and down-to-earth man by nature. And while Otto came to Greece, intoxicated by the romanticism of Munich, to fulfill his father's wishes and visions, George accepted the Greek throne despite the objections of his family, who did not want him to abandon his right to the throne of Denmark and were fully aware, as was George himself (to the extent any youth of 17 could be), of the uncertain situation in which Greece found itself and the problems he would face. As it turned out, however, that George had Greek politicians around him in place of the Bavarian clique that surrounded Otto helped him to acclimatise to his new country rapidly and to adopt its customs as far as possible.

In this, he was helped substantially by Queen Olga, who, though she had grown up in the Russian court, retained the simplicity and optimism of her youth. Olga had never dreamed of being queen; indeed, a few months before her marriage at the age of 16, she wrote to her tutor, Rosalie Possiet: "Happily, I am not yet queen, though unfortunately I will become a queen one day! But I do not care; when you have someone like my Willy –as she called George I– you can easily put up with everything". Yet, she carried out her duties successfully and sensitively, and became the most popular queen in the history of Greece. That she had been raised in the Orthodox faith helped her understand the Greek people, who were so devoted to their creed and its profound links with the idea of a 'homeland'. Indeed, Olga was the first queen since the foundation of the Greek monarchy to be addressed as "Most Pious" by the Metropolitan Bishop of Athens from the Royal Doors of Athens Cathedral – an epithet he had refused to apply to Otto, Amalia or George I himself, all of whom belonged to other Christian denominations.

With the exception of the palace Gärtner built for Otto, then, all the other 'palaces' that were built or converted were nothing more than small country villas,

considerably smaller than those erected by the Greek bourgeoisie of today in Athens' suburbs and in summer resorts around the country. In fact, the royal villas simply catered to the life of what was an ordinary large, bourgeois family during the summer months.

It should be noted at this point that this appears to be the result of conscious decisions taken both by the first governor of Greece, Ioannis Kapodistrias, and later by the family of George I, though possibly not for the same reasons.

This view is confirmed by the differences between the two large palaces on Corfu: the palace of Saints Michael and George and the Achilleion.

What set these royal country villas apart were the large estates in which they stood, the dense vegetation and the greenery. The creation of small farming and stock-raising units on Corfu and at Tatoi (and earlier at Eptalofos) were essentially a reflection of similar complexes maintained by kings and nobles in the rest of Europe, and the last remnants of the feudal society which had long since been effaced by the centuries of Turkish rule – for Greeks, at least, for there were large Turkish estates [çiflikler] in mainland Greece and elsewhere.

After the final abolition of Greece's constitutional monarchy, the royal property was gradually and largely transferred to the Greek state, which is now under an obligation to maintain, conserve and exploit it to the benefit of the Greek people, and to preserve its historical memory and tradition as impartially as possible for the generations to come. For, as Nietzsche said, "the people with the longest memory will enjoy the longest future".

*Friedrich von Gärtner. Decorative design for the Athens palace. Munich. State Drawing and Print Collection.*

# BIBLIOGRAPHY

About E., *La Grèce contemporaine* (in Greek), Tolidis, Athens, n.d.

Agathos, S., *Τα απομνημονεύματα του Κάιζερ Γουλιέλμου II, Αναμνήσεις από την Κέρκυρα*, Corfu, n.d.

Aliberti, S, *Αμαλία η Βασίλισσα της Ελλάδος*, n.p., Athens, 1896.

Avril N., *Elisabeth of Austria* (in Greek), Okeanida, Athens, 1995.

Baedeker, K., *Greece. Handbook for Travellers*, Leipzig 1894.

–, *Grèce. Manuel du voyageur*, Baedeker, Leipzig & Paris, 1910.

Bastea, E., *Αθήνα 1834-1896, Νεοκλασική πολεοδομία και ελληνική εθνική συνείδηση*, Libro, Athens, 2008.

Bickford-Smith, R.A.H., *Greece under King George* (in Greek), Ermis, Athens, 1993.

Biris, K., *Τα πρώτα σχέδια των Αθηνών, ιστορία και ανάλυσίς των*, n.p., Athens 1933.

–, *Αθηναϊκαί Μελέται*, issue I (1938).

–, "Ο Κλέντσε στας Αθήνας", *Nea Estia* (Christmas 1940).

Bofilias, A., *Κτήμα Επταλόφου και Πύργος Βασιλίσσης, Η βασίλισσα Αμαλία 1818-1875*, n.p., n.d.

Bouse, V., "Από χθες φυτεύω φοίνικες. Ο Εθνικός Κήπος", *Kathimerini*, 17 April 2003.

Bremer, F., *Η Ελλάδα και οι Έλληνες την εποχή του Όθωνα*, Katoptro, Athens, 2002.

Conte Corti, E.C., *Ludwig I. von Bayern, Ein Ringen um Freiheit, Schönheit und Liebe*, Bruckmann, Munich, 1942.

Demenegi-Viriraki, Aik., *Παλαιά Ανάκτορα Αθηνών 1836-1986* [Athens' old palaces], Technical Chamber of Greece, Athens, 1994.

–, *Παλαιά Ανάκτορα Αθηνών 1887-2000, Συμπλήρωμα στο βιβλίο Παλαιά Ανάκτορα Αθηνών 1836-1986*, Technical Chamber of Greece, Athens, 1994.

–, *Παλαιά Ανάκτορα Αθηνών. Το κτίριο της Βουλής των Ελλήνων*, Hellenic Parliament, Athens, 2007.

Demosthenopoulou, E., *Öffentliche Bauten unter König Otto um Athen*, Diss., Munich, 1970.

Deros, I., Βιογραφία ελληνικής βασιλικής οικογένειας, n.p., n.d.

Dorovinis, V., "Συμβολές στην ιστορία της κτιριοδομίας της καποδιστριακής εποχής. Η κατοικία του Καποδίστρια και το Παλάτιον ή Κυβερνείον", *Archaiologia* 43-44 (1992).

Durand, J.N.L., *Précis des leçons d'architecture données à l'Ecole Polytechnique*, Chez l'auteur, Paris, 1802-1805.

Eleb-Vidal, M. – Debarre-Blanchard, A., *Architecture de la vie privée XVIIe-XIXe*, Archives de l'Architecture Moderne, Brussels, 1989.

Evangelidis, T., *Ιστορία του Όθωνος*, n.p., Athens, 1893.

Ficker, Fr., *Ernst Ziller. Ein sächsischer Architekt und Bauforscher in Griechenland*, Josef Fink, Lindenberg im Allgäu, 2003.

Fleming, J., *Adam and his Circle*, John Murray, London, 1962.

Fotiadis, D., *Όθων, Η μοναρχία*, Kypseli, Athens, 1963.

Furneaux-Jordan, R., *A concise history of Western architecture* (in Greek), Ypodomi, Athens, 1981.

Gatopoulos, D., *Η ιστορία της αθηναϊκής κοινωνίας*, Aetos, Athens, 1942.

Georgievna, M. Grand Duchess of Russia, *Αναμνήσεις της βασιλόπαιδος Μαρίας*, Alfa I.M. Skaziki, Athens, n.d.

Georgiou-Nilsen, M., *Η Ελλάδα του Άντερσεν*, Patakis, Athens, 1997.

Glenis, *Ενθυμίων των αειμνήστων Βασιλέων Γεωργίου Α' – Όλγας – Κωνσταντίνου ΙΒ' – Σοφίας – Αλεξάνδρου και βασιλοπαίδων Αλεξάνδρας και Όλγας*, exhib. cat., George I Museum, Athens, 1936.

Gould Lee, A., *The Royal House of Greece*, Ward Lock & Co., London, 1948.

*Handbuch der Architektur: Die Garten-Architektur*, Stuttgart, 1999.

Hederer, O., *Klassizismus*, Heyne, Munich, 1982.

Heidenreuther, R. et al., *Ein Griechischer Traum, Leo von Klenze der Archäologe*, exhib. cat., Glyptothek München, Munich, 1986.

Kaiser Wilhelm II, *Erinnerungen an Korfu*, W. de Gruyter & Co., Berlin-Leipzig, 1924.

Karatza, G.M., *Ο παλιός καθρέφτης. Εικόνες από την εποχή του Όθωνα*, Ikaros, Athens, 1970.

Kardamitsi-Adami, M. – Biris M., *Νεοκλασική Αρχιτεκτονική στην Ελλάδα*, Melissa, Athens, 2001.

Kardamitsi-Adami, M. – Papanikolaou-Christensen, A., *Ernst Ziller, Αναμνήσεις*, Libro, Athens, 1997.

Kardamitsi-Adami, M., "Τα κυβερνητικά κτίρια. Ιωάννης Καποδίστριας", *Kathimerini*, 25-26 March 1995.

–, *Το Α' εν Αθήναις Γυμνάσιον – Ένα σχολείο σε αναζήτηση στέγης. Αι Αθήναι ως εκπαιδευτική πόλις από τον 19ο προς τον 20ό αιώνα*, University of Athens / Educational History Museum / Municipality of Athens Cultural Organization, Athens, 1999.

–, "Η κατάσταση στο Ναύπλιο στις αρχές του 1833", *Navpliaka Analekta*, vol. IV, Municipality of Nafplio, 2000.

–, "Ο κήπος και οι Αθηναίοι. Ο Εθνικός Κήπος", *Kathimerini*, 17 April 2003.

–, "Το Ανάκτορο της Τρίπολης και οι αρχιτέκτονες Γεράσιμος και Αναστάσης Μεταξάς" in *Λαμπηδών: Αφιέρωμα στη μνήμη της Ντούλας Μουρίκη*, National Technical University of Athens, Athens, 2003.

–, *Τα προάστια της Αθήνας τον 19ο αιώνα, Χωρίς όρια οι αχανείς εκτάσεις των αθηναϊκών προαστίων*, Futura, Athens, 2003.

–, *Η Αθήνα και οι Αθηναίοι. Η Αθήνα στα τέλη του 19ου αιώνα. Οι Πρώτοι Διεθνείς Ολυμπιακοί Αγώνες*, Historical and Ethnological Society of Greece, Athens, 2004.

–, *Ερνστ Τσίλλερ 1837-1923, Η τέχνη του κλασικού*, Melissa, Athens, 2006.

–, *Νέα στοιχεία για τα πρώτα προσωρινά ανάκτορα του Όθωνα και τον κήπο τους, Λάμπρος Ευταξίας, ο βίος και η πολιτεία ενός Ευπατρίδη*, Kaktos/Museum of the City of Athens, Athens, 2006.

Karolou, I., *Όλγα η Βασίλισσα των Ελλήνων*, Estia, Athens, 1934.

Kolonas, V., *Η εκτός των τειχών επέκταση της Θεσσαλονίκης. Εικονογραφία της συνοικίας Χαμηδιέ (1885-1912)*, Ph.D. thesis, Department of Architecture, Aristotle University of Thessaloniki, Thessaloniki, 1991.

Koromilas, L., *Το αθηναϊκό κελάρυσμα*, Greek Water Company, Athens, 1977.

Kostis, C.N., *Αναμνήσεις εκ της Αυλής Γεωργίου του Α'*, n.p., Athens, 1949.

Kotsowilis, K., *Die Griechenbegeisterung der Bayern unter Otto I.*, n.p., Munich, 2007.

*Leo von Klenze* (collective volume), Munich, 1963.

Koumarianou, Aik., *Αθήνα. Η πόλη – οι άνθρωποι – αφηγήσεις και μαρτυρίες, 12ος-19ος αιώνας*, Potamos, Athens, 2005.

Kyriaki, S., *Η έπαυλη Mon Repos στην Κέρκυρα*, Hellenic Ministry of Culture/Archaeological Receipts Fund, Athens, 2006.

Laios, G., *Ο Πύργος της Βασιλίσσης*, n.p., Athens 1977.

Levidis, N., "Ο Βασιλεύς Όθων εν Κηφισία" [King Otto in Kifissia], reprint from the Historical and Ethnological Society of Greece Bulletin, vol. I (New Series), Athens, 1930.

Linner, S., *Μία Σουηδέζα στην Ελλάδα του 19ου αιώνα*, Proskinio, Athens, 1998.

Lutt, C., *Μία δανέζα στην Αυλή του Όθωνα*, translated, edited and annotated by A. Papanikolaou-Christensen, Ermis, Athens, 1981.

–, *Στην Αθήνα του 1847-1848*, translated, edited and annotated by A. Papanikolaou-Christensen, Ermis, Athens, 1981.

Malagara, A. – Stratidakis, Ch., *Ιστορία του Ελληνικού Έθνους*, vol. XII, XIII.

Markezinis, S., *Πολιτική Ιστορία της Ελλάδας*, Papyros, Athens 1973-1974.

Mauer, G.L., *Ο ελληνικός λαός (Heidelberg 1835)*, Tolidis, Athens, 1976.

Meyers Reisebücher, *Griechenland*, Meyers, Leipzig-Vienna, 1901.

Middleton, R. – Watkin, D., *Neoclassical and 19th-century architecture*, vols. 1-2, Electra/Rizzoli, New York, 1980.

Moningen, H., *Friedrich von Gärtner, Original Pläne und Studien*, n.p., Munich, 1882.

Murken, J., *König Otto von Griechenland, Museum der Gemeinde Ottobrunn*, Weltkunst Verlag, Munich, 1995.

Niemann, G. – Felge,F., *Theophilus Hansen und seine Werke*, n.p., Vienna, 1893.

Nordenflycht, Julie (von), "Επιστολαί Κυρίας της τιμής εν Αθήναις προς φίλην της εν Γερμανία, 1837-1842", translated by K. Tsaousopoulou, *Historical and Ethnological Society of Greece Bulletin*, 1922.

Palaska-Papastathi, E., *Αχίλλειο. Ιστορία και θρύλος*, Corfu, 1992.

–, "Το Ανάκτορο των Αγίων Μιχαήλ και Γεωργίου", *Kathimerini*, Athens, 1966.

–, "Το περίφημο Αχίλλειο", *Kathimerini*, Athens, 1966.

Papageorgiou-Venetas, A., "Ο Φρειδερίκος Γκαίρτνερ στην Ελλάδα και η οικοδόμηση των ανακτόρων των Αθηνών", *Archaiologia* 49 (1993).

–, *Αθήνα: ένα όραμα του κλασικισμού* [Athens, a vision of classicism], Kapon, Athens, 2001.

–, *Ο κήπος της Αμαλίας*, Ikaros, Athens, 2008.

Papadopoulos-Vrettos, M., *Αι νέαι Αθήναι* [La nouvelle Athènes], n.p., Athens, 1860.

Papadopoulou-Symeonidou, P., *Η επιλογή της Αθήνας ως πρωτεύουσας της Ελλάδος, 1833-1834*, Kyriakidis, Thessaloniki, 1996.

Papanikolaou, M., *Η εικονογράφηση του Μεγάρου της Βουλής*, Hellenic Parliament, Athens, 1998.

Papanikolaou-Christensen, A. (trans., ed., notes), *Γεώργιος Α, Φίλτατε, Επιστολές από την Ελλάδα, 1897-1913*, Ermis, Athens, 2006.

Papanikolaou-Christensen, A. (trans., ed., notes), *Χριστιανός Χάνσεν, Επιστολές και Σχέδια από την Ελλάδα*, Okeanida, Athens, 1993.

Papantoniou, Z., *Όθωνας* (3rd edn.), Estia, Athens, 1997.

Papastamos, D., *Ε. Τσίλλερ, Προσπάθεια μονογραφίας*, Ministry of Culture and Science, Athens, 1973.

Philippides, D., *Νεοκλασικές πόλεις στην Ελλάδα (1830-1920)*, Melissa, Athens, 2007.

Prince Nicholas of Greece, *Τα πενήντα χρόνια της ζωής μου*, Greka, Athens, 1926.

Raabyemagle H. – Smidt C.M., *Classicism in Copenhagen*, Gyldendal, København, 1998.

Reiser, R., *Klenzes geheime Memoiren*, Buchendorfer Verlag, Munich, 2004.

Riemann G. – Heese Chr., *Karl Friedrich Schinkel. Architekturzeichnungen*, Henschel Verlag, Berlin, 1996.

Risasen, G.T., *Slottet, Kongelig Stil Gjennom 150ar*, Forlaged Geelmuyclen-Kiese, Oslo, 1998.

Russack, H.H., *Deutsche bauen in Athen* (in Greek), Govostis, Athens, n.d.

Seidl, W., *Bayern in Griechenland: Die Geschichte eines Abenteuers* (in Greek), Elliniki Evroekdotiki, Athens, 1984.

Skarpia-Heupel, X., *Η μορφολογία του γερμανικού κλασικισμού (1789-1848) και η δημιουργική αφομοίωσή του από την ελληνική αρχιτεκτονική (1833-1897)*, Aristotle University of Thessaloniki, Thessaloniki, 1976.

Stamatopoulos, K., *Το Χρονικό του Τατοϊου* [The chronicle of Tatoi], Kapon, Athens, 2004.

Stefanou, S., *Οι γάμοι του Διαδόχου*, n.p., n.d.

*Τα Ανέκδοτα του Βασιλέως Γεωργίου του Α'* n.p., n.d.

Stahl, Fr., *Schinkel, Piererschen Hofbuchdruckerei*, Stephan Geibel und Co., Altenburg, 1911.

Steffen, R., *Das neue Hellas. Griechen und Bayern zur Zeit Ludwigs I.*, Hirmer, Bayerisches Nationalmuseum, Munich, 2000.

–, *Leben in Griechenland 1834 und 1835. Bettina Schinas geb. von Savigny Briefe und Berichte an ihre Eltern in Berlin*, Lienau, Munster, 2002.

Stillman, D., *English Neoclassical Architecture*, W. Zwemmer, London, 1988.

Tamvakis, N., *Κατάλογος καλλωπιστικών φυτών Εθνικού Κήπου με σύντομη περιγραφή της εξέλιξης και της κηποτεχνικής μορφής του*, Committee of Public Gardens, Athens, 1981.

Tsantaridis, G., *Mon Repos*, Ellinoekdotiki, Athens, 1994.

Tsokopoulos, G., "Η ζωή εις τα Ανάκτορα των Αθηνών", *Panathinaia*, Athens, n.d.

Urwin, D., *Νεοκλασικισμός*, Athens, Kastaniotis, 1999.

Zaousis, Al., *Αμαλία και Όθωνας*, Okeanida, Athens, 2000.

Zernioti-Vergi, D, *Mon Repos. Οι αρχαιότητες – η έπαυλη – ο κήπος*, Apostrofos, Corfu, 2002.

### Exhibition catalogues, collective and other volumes

*1781-1841, Schinkel, l'architetto del principe* (collective volume), Abrizzi Editore, Venice, 1982.

*Friedrich von Gärtner 1791-1847, Leben-Werk-Schüler* (collective volume), Prestel Verlag, Munich, 1976.

*Friedrich von Gärtner ein Architektenleben 1791-1847* (collective volume), Klinkhardt & Niermann, Munich, 1992.

*Αθήνα-Μόναχο, Τέχνη και πολιτισμός στη νέα Ελλάδα*, exhib. cat., Greek National Gallery – A. Soutzos Museum, Athens, 2000.

*Αθηναϊκός Νεοκλασικισμός* (collective volume), Municipality of Athens Cultural Centre, Athens, 1996.

*Από την Αθήνα στη Βαμβέργη. Η ζωή του πρώτου βασιλικού ζεύγους της Ελλάδος Όθωνος και Αμαλίας μετά το 1862*, exhib. cat., Museum of the City of Athens, Athens, 2005.

*Έκθεσις Σχεδίων Αρχείου Αρχιτέκτονος Ερνέστου Τσίλλερ (1837-1923) και Σχεδίων Αρχιτέκτονος Θεόφιλου Χάνσεν (1811-1891)*, exhib. cat., Stratigopoulos Hall, Athens, 1939.

*Η βασίλισσα Αμαλία, 1818-1875*, exhib. cat., Museum of the City of Athens, Athens, 2007.

*Ο Βασιλεύς Κωνσταντίνος*, Sub-ministry of the Press and Tourism, Athens, 1939.

*Οι τοιχογραφίες του Μεγάρου της Βουλής*, Hellenic Parliament, Athens, 2007.

*Ρέθυμνο Κρήτη, Οδηγός για την πόλη*, n.p. Athens, 1995.

*Τα 75 χρόνια της Ελληνικής Δυναστείας*, Sub-ministry of the Press and Tourism, Athens, 1948.

PHOTOGRAPHS:

YIORGIS YEROLYMBOS: ILLUS. 27, 28, 31-33, 58, 60, 64, 71, 74-79, 81, 85-91, 105-108, 110, 120, 121, 127, 131-141, 163, 171, 187, 188, 191-200, 202, 205, 209-213, 215, 248, 251, 252, 254, 256-260, 263, 268-280, 286-292, 298-306, 324, 325, 330-332, 334, 336, 338, 339, 341-347

(THE CAPTIONS PERTAINING TO PHOTOGRAPHS TAKEN FOR THIS VOLUME INCLUDE THE CURRENT NAME OF THE BUILDINGS OR SPACES IN BRACKETS).

ELIAS ELIADIS: DRAWINGS AND MAPS FROM THE BENAKI MUSEUM AND THE NATIONAL HISTORICAL MUSEUM.

THALIA KIBARI: ILLUS. 50, 51, 61, 62, 63, 65-69, 72, 73, 93, 216, 219-223